SAILING CRAFT

SAILING CRAFT

by

Frank Rosenow

SAIL BOOKS

BOSTON

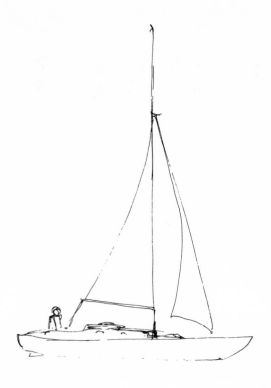

Book design by William Gilkerson

Library of Congress Cataloging in Publication Data

Rosenow, Frank, 1944-
  Sailing Craft.

  1. Sailboats. 2. Rosenow, Frank, 1944-
I. Title.
VM351.R67 1982   623.8′223   82-10423
ISBN 0-914814-33-8

BST

Contents

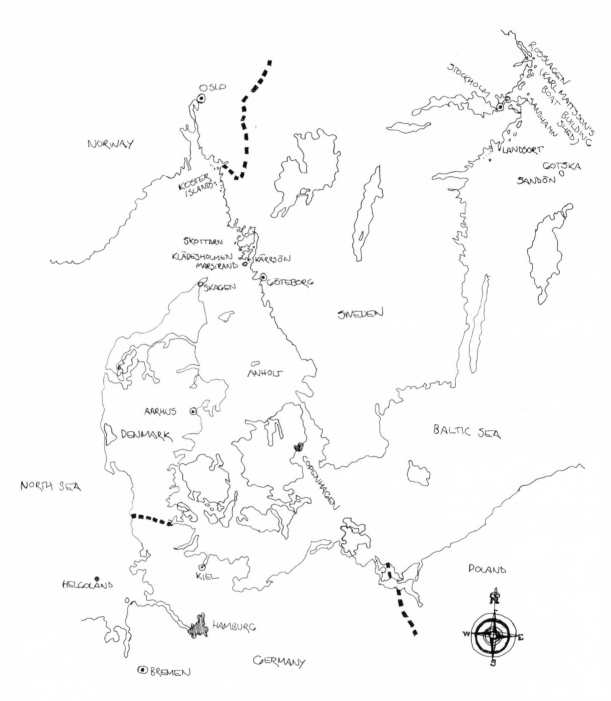

OSLO

NORWAY

KOSTER
ISLANDS

SKOTTARN
KLÄDESHOLMEN
MARSTRAND

KÄRRSÖN

SKAGEN

GÖTEBORG

SWEDEN

ANHOLT

AARHUS

DENMARK

COPENHAGEN

BALTIC SEA

NORTH SEA

HELGOLAND

KIEL

HAMBURG

BREMEN

GERMANY

POLAND

STOCKHOLM

ROSLAGEN
(KARL MATTSON'S
BOAT BUILDING
SHED)

SANDHAMN

LANDSORT

GOTSKA
SANDÖN

N
W   E
S

* GENERAL MAP OF
SCANDINAVIAN WATERS *

Introduction

These sketches of people and sailing craft owe their existence to Marstrand, the small Swedish island facing the North Sea where I grew up. The sea was our open road and provided us our livelihood of fresh mackerel and cod, which was rock-salted to last through the year.

Here boats were built lapstrake, from native pine or oak, in wooden sheds. The simple ekas (*ek* means "oak" in Swedish, and *eka* can be interpreted as something made from that wood) were fitted with cotton spritsails. In the building and using of these boats, there lay an intuitive craft and an honesty of purpose that we young ones were given some sense of.

Looking back at those times, I have tried to record glimpses of the great changes that have occurred in the design and construction of sailboats. The use of natural materials like wood, cotton, and hemp, has largely been replaced by synthetics like Dacron and fiberglass. The building of single boats to the traditional designs by tiny shops has given way to mass production. The Pelle Petterson boat I am sailing as this is written has a forty-page instruction book in addition to separate manuals on the engine, winches and other installations.

Sailing Craft deals with another kind of boat, a boat that speaks for her owner with greater eloquence than can the product of any production line. These boats, whether large or small, were created as much by intuition as by science and constructed according to the unique experience of individual builders. The book also records some of the debts that the sport of sailing in general, and I in particular, owes to individuals possessed of a certain kind of courage. It may be an old man's courage in trusting a bunch of children with a boat, or it may be a young man's pluck in breaking with the old rules of sailboat design as he faces what designer Peter Norlin once described as "that awesome blank paper."

In *Sailing Craft*, I have also tried to record something of the timeless meaning that small boats have for those who sail them. Some years ago, I sought shelter from a summer gale by sailing my boat *Chief* under the outlying Landsort Light in the Baltic Sea. I maneuvered through a narrow opening to a rock-pool shelter west of the light tower. It was near midnight, but my lines were taken by a young fellow from a curious-looking, obviously homemade 18-foot sailboat already at rest under the high, wind-cutting rocks.

At dawn, he got underway, steering for the outlying island of Gotska Sandön. He gave me a friendly wave as he settled down over the tiller he had fashioned from a broomstick. The boat was obviously homemade of Masonite and plywood covered here and there with patches of fiberglass. In the ugly swell left over by the gale, the battens made deep creases in the sails, which looked like they had been cut on the kitchen table from bedsheets.

And yet . . . who can fathom that skipper's joy as he trimmed his sheets and set his course?

ROSENOW

Marstrand, Sweden
August 1982

Svennungsson's Eka

Back in 1949, my grandfather Konrad Rutgersson of Marstrand, on the west coast of Sweden, ordered a 14-foot eka from his near neighbor August Svennungsson. These cheaply built, able little craft were at that time prevalent in every nautical household along the coast, and Svennungsson could rest on a centuries-old building tradition for the general type. With a boatbuilding experience of his own that went back to 1893, he lofted her up from inside his head, relying on his *ögonmått* (literally "eye measure," but the expression is a rich one in Swedish boatbuilding, denoting a craft of hand and eye that goes beyond the simple taking of a measure) to shape the hull fair and true. He also took into account the bending dictates of his pine wood planks and the eka's projected use as a knockabout boat.

Starting from a backbone keel plank set up in his waterfront building shop, he built her up lapstrake, with ten wide pine wood planks on simple, sawn pine frames. To fasten the planks together at the overlap, he used copper rivets, which gave an advantage in building speed compared with the traditional, jammed-fast juniper trunnels. For the rest, he used only natural materials, which he worked with the basic hand tools.

At the end of a week, the boat left Svennungsson's workshed in exchange for 175 kronor (thirty-five dollars, approximately) and was launched. A wide, stable craft, she sat jauntily on the water, her planks providing a naturally graceful sheer line that emphasized the snout bow, the brave angle of the sternpost, and the elevated curve

1

ASH .SOLE

WEDGE

of the transom. A fresh coat of oil-based white paint on the hull and of emerald green paint on the thwarts and floorboards gave her a distinct personality compared with other Svennungsson ekas around Marstrand. Most were finished bright with a mixture of linseed oil and turpentine. Even without its colorful paint job, our eka would have stood out from those hundreds of others built by different builders. Any of the waterfront boys who grew up with me can still pick out a Svennungsson eka in a busy harbor. If there is any small doubt about a particular eka's origin, the boat in question usually turns out to have been built by the old man's son, Bror, in later years.

The main thwart of the eka had a hole in it for a mast, and Konrad lost little time in making one for his boat, together with a sprit boom and a home-sewn, loose-footed cotton main and jib and pintle-hung rudder. Traditionally, the boats were sailed off the wind and sculled or rowed to windward or in a calm.

Konrad's modifications completed the sailing craft that was to carry my three cousins, my older brother, and me into an under-standing of the delicate balances ruling the boating life of the islands. At first glance, the improvement in our fiber was scant. While before we had roamed the meadows of the main islands, chasing cows and starting brush fires, we now raided the gull colonies and sheep herds on small, outlying islands. The eka was a means of obtaining a freedom close to anarchy. Nothing was sacred except, because of their obvious rarity, the warm, darkly mottled eggs of the brown eider duck. Our sport was to throw seagull eggs at sheep and at parties of picnicking Marstrand summer lodgers. We usually ended up panting for breath, half-choked with laughter, hiding in a heather-filled gully among the rocks. We did not always escape retribution, though.

One morning in May we set out for the large gull colony on Rammholmen Island where the eggs had been laid but were not yet hatched. As we tied up the eka in the natural rock harbor on the island's east side, the gulls, which numbered in the thousands, were already rising angrily. Scouring Rammholmen from one end to another, walking abreast and smashing eggs, we heard the noise of

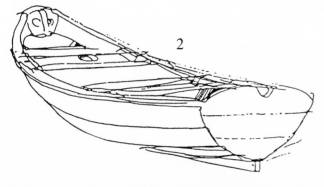

2

SVENNUNGSSON SHEER LINES:
THE BASIC EKA

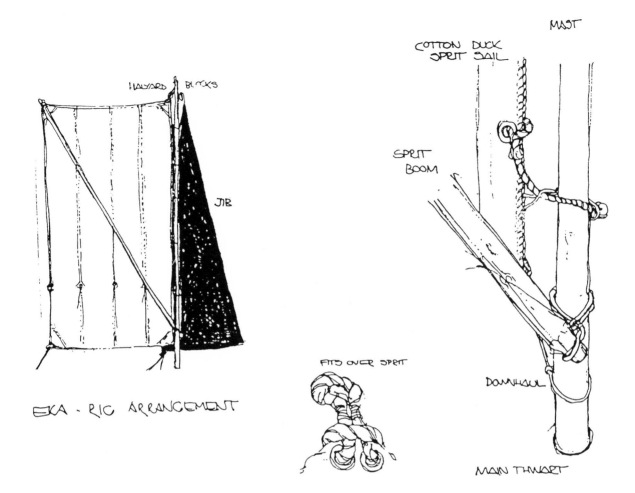

HALYARD BLOCKS

JIB

EKA - RIG ARRANGEMENT

FITS OVER SPRIT

COTTON DUCK
SPRIT SAIL

MAST

SPRIT
BOOM

DOWNHAUL

MAIN THWART

the gulls hovering overhead increase in pitch, and we had to look out for droppings and sham attacks.

Lars, my brown-haired, gentle-eyed cousin ("the boy has his mother's eyes," our aunts used to say), was at the highest point of the island, trying to throw an egg as far as the island light, when a furious gull parent dive-bombed the side of his head—following up with his full weight rather than veering off at the last instant as we had come to expect. The blow dazed the bird and impaired Lars's hearing for years to come, and after that event we took to dropping adroitly to the ground whenever we heard a rush of wings over the breakers.

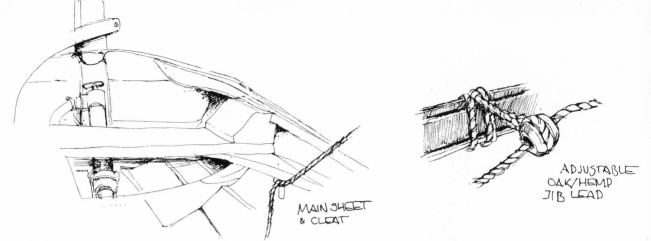

MAIN SHEET & CLEAT

ADJUSTABLE OAK/HEMP JIB LEAD

Learning to sail the eka came as naturally. Lars and my brother, Benjy, my elders by five years, had already been out cod fishing with Konrad in his twenty-odd-foot double-ender, which was built traditionally with lapstrake oak planks on grown oak frames and fitted with a slow turning one-cylinder engine and a steadying sail. By putting the two boys on the tiller, with an occasional warning, *Det lever i seglet* ("You're high," or literally, "The sail is alive"), and by simply having them around where they could observe and imitate knot-tying and splicing, he had let them absorb boathandling practices.

For the younger lot of relations, Sven, Göran, and me, Konrad had built foot-long, white-painted sailboat models with lead keels and self-tacking gaff rigs. For years, we sailed them in the island wash pond, a body of water in which we could conveniently reach with a long stick any craft in irons or becalmed. What difference, then, did the eka make?

I believe that on a deep and lasting level, Svennungsson's eka taught us more things than I can enumerate, or even know. She was the first real tool we knew, and she sharpened her crew by her very limitations. Ashore, we used to amble along as chance took us, but under sail, we paid attention. We had to. The lack of a proper keel made the eka (she remained without a name, as is common with small, all-purpose boats in these islands) lose more than she gained on many a current-plagued windward leg. For the same reason— she had merely a rubbing strake as an excuse for a keel—coming about invariably meant backing the jib and praying with the helm down as she lost way or even began to back up. A bit of sculling with the rudder or an oar was often needed to bring her about.

4

Since she was such a cow to windward and outboards were a luxury we could not afford, we had to master alternative methods of propulsion. Straight rowing in a slow, measured stroke came easily enough, after you knew how to keep the oar between the juniper thole pins, but feathering the blades, as every seamanlike islander took care to do, was slow in coming. Single-oar sculling from a standing position was the hardest skill of all to master since the unballasted oar kept coming back at you from the notch in the eka's stern.

After a squall or wet sail, her sails had to be spread out and dried to avoid the quick appearance of black mold spots in the canvas. In spring, she had to be scraped and put in the water early unless we covered her with old home-woven rugs dunked in water. Otherwise, her lapstraked seams would gape open in the sunshine. In addition, the necessity of knowing how to tie a *halvslag* ("double half hitch") or *pålstek* ("bowline") presented itself very clearly since anything less securely contrived would not keep the eka in her berth on a rough autumn night.

In addition to the automatic rewards of keeping up with such natural demands, there was a special joy in fitting our backs to the curve of the sun-baked frames inside the boat, our eyes close to the level of the sea, and watching the waves come in to lift the buoyant hull and feeling its response against our bodies.

Konrad said little about our use of the eka, attending to his cotton flatfish nets and line fishing from the double-ender, along with summer and lay-up work on the big yachts. Unlike our other elders, he never denied us the eka and must have had complete faith in our coming to terms with her and vice versa, regardless of wind and weather. Konrad might, I suppose, have built the eka himself, in the

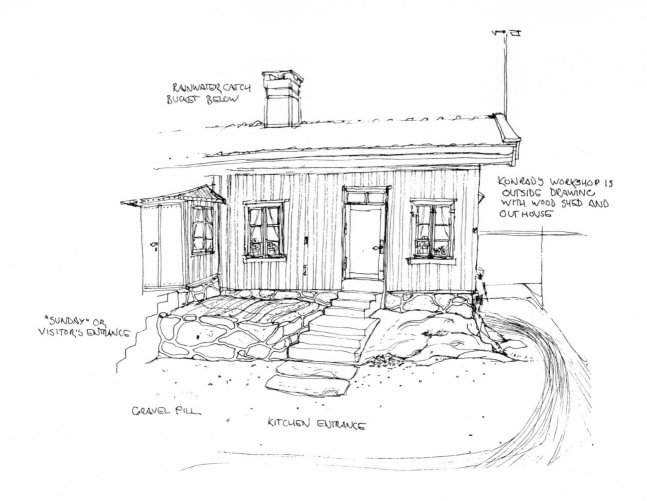

RAINWATER CATCH
BUCKET BELOW

KONRAD'S WORKSHOP IS
OUTSIDE DRAWING
WITH WOOD SHED AND
OUT HOUSE

"SUNDAY" OR
VISITOR'S ENTRANCE

GRAVEL FILL

KITCHEN ENTRANCE

DRIED BUTTERCUPS

same careful way that he had fashioned the two houses in our sunny, sea-front compound and inside one, the fine-grained, tan-and-gold oak chest with dove-tailed drawers. But he had recognized Sven-nungsson's gift and experience in making a "right" boat, and right she was.

In the end—that is, after eighteen years—the eka passed from active service. Having aged beautifully, as natural materials do, for some years, her planks opened up so badly one spring that there was obviously no lust for life on the water in her any more. For a few more years, she lay bottom-up on some rocks near the harbor, a silvery skeleton of greater beauty even than in her prime. Then, a new generation of boys broke her brittle back, and her timbers spread gently over the neighborhood of her birthplace.

6

The Paid Hand

The idea of sailing as a way to pass the time of day was only reluctantly accepted by Konrad Rutgersson. As the eldest of eleven children born to the farming and fishing household of Johan Rutgersson at the end of the nineteenth century, he had to help with the breadwinning fight right from his childhood.

The family island, Kärrsön, which lay across from the Hättan pilot station in the Hake Fjord not far from Marstrand, had to be paid for from what the meager pastures and the windmill Johan built overlooking the sea could be made to yield. At six, Konrad was given the task of rowing the family eka across to the red-and-white pilot cottages on Hättan with the morning milk, and it was not long before he routinely went out before sun-up in the big double-ender to trail lines for mackerel and check crab nets and lobster pots.

It was only after he had grown up, married the school teacher on the next island, and moved to Marstrand that he had much opportunity to see pleasure boats. Apart from King Oscar II's rakish white steam yacht *Drott* and one or two R Class sailing boats owned by wealthy summer visitors, the common boats in the islands were the traditional native double-enders. Of these sailing work boats, a variety originating on the northernmost of the Koster Islands—the boats were called Kosters—became the most refined.

The sailing Kosters (some were motorized, with only a steadying sail left to show their lineage) were tubby double-enders with lapstraked hulls, great loose-footed gaff sails, and enormous load capacity. Their easily handled small jibs were sheeted from the cockpit by hand tackles, and because this rig did not call for much crew movement on deck, high bulwarks, stanchions, and pulpits were deemed unnecessary. They were humble rigs, with short, easily handled and repaired bits of spars set on the stubby, firmly anchored mast. The tarred cordage, twine, and plough-steel wire they utilized were readily available all along the coast. In every detail, they were "folk boats," relating to the resources of their time and place. Their use was mainly in the interisland transportation of goods and people, and even sheep. On the Marstrand waterfront,

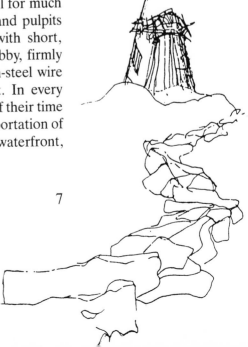

7

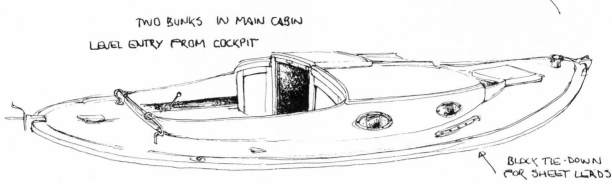

SMALL, 1930'S KOSTER

TWO BUNKS IN MAIN CABIN

LEVEL ENTRY FROM COCKPIT

BLOCK TIE-DOWN
FOR SHEET LEADS

some old fishermen used them to take out summer visitors for pleasure sails on the fjord.

Konrad stayed with his fishing and some merchant marine sailing to scrape together cash for his growing family. But at the end of World War One, a Göteborg shipowner, Gösta Dahlman, brought the 77-foot R boat *Mariska* to Marstrand and asked Konrad to form a five-man crew to race her. *Mariska* was a 15-Meter designed and built in 1907 by William Fife of Fairlee, Scotland. Her waterline length was 53 feet, her beam was 14 feet, and her draft was 11 feet. With the topsail set, she spread 3,443 square feet of Egyptian cotton canvas. Her Fife sheer and the prospect of extra money induced Konrad to put himself, his teenage son Conny, and three more locals in dark blue *Mariska* jerseys and white duck trousers. He never regretted the decision. Racing the boat in the Round Kattegatt Race (a precursor of the present Skaw Race), he soon earned the race-winning bonus of a gold watch. A matching chain quickly followed, along with regular pay.

Per Carlsson, the son of Gunnar Carlsson, owner of Konrad's later command, the skerry cruiser *Kratos,* told me of this episode—gleaned from his father—on *Mariska* in the Kattegatt race. "*Mariska* was racing downwind against a German 15-Meter. It was blowing around 25 knots, and *Mariska,* which Konrad had rigged for reliability, trailed the German, whose gear was filed down to the last ounce. Whatever the *Mariska* crew did, she remained a hundred yards behind the German, and the finish was not far away.

CONNY

8

"Konrad finally told the skipper, 'I think we should set the topsail.' Given the conditions, the owner thought that suggestion crazy, but Konrad's reputation for sound judgment was such that he shrugged his shoulders. 'If you can find anyone to climb the mast, go ahead.' Konrad and Conny climbed up and set the topsail, loose and twisting. They were hardly back on deck when the Germans set theirs. Konrad watched them. A gust came through, and the spar on the German broke in splinters and toppled. 'I was waiting for that,' Konrad said."

Mariska was sold to one of Dahlman's business rivals, Karl Mattiesen, known as the Banana King ever since he had made a fortune by shipping green bananas to Sweden. With *Mariska*'s sale, Konrad became a skipper for another shipowner named Gunnar Carlsson. Not content with summer work on yachts, he also shipped as "boss man" on one of Carlsson's steamers, sending home letters from a variety of places, including one that was later to have some real meaning for me—Australia. Wherever he went, he was a keen observer of local sailing craft, and each summer, he practiced his finely developed racing skills.

In the summer of 1930, at the Sandhamn jubilee regatta of the Royal Swedish Sailing Society, Konrad sailed the 8-Meter R boat *Cagg* for a consortium of west coast yachtsmen that included Carlsson. It was there that he first saw *Kratos*. Said Per Carlsson, "It was in the midst of the depression, and everyone had to tighten his belt. There was no fuel, and many boats were laid up. By chance, Konrad saw *Kratos* and realized that another dry year or two would finish her. When the races were over, he came back to Göteborg and went to see my father. 'I have seen a boat that you should buy,' he said. 'How much do they want for it,' my father asked. 'Five thousand kronor,' Konrad said. We bought her, on his word, although times were bad for us, too.

"She had been built at the famous Neglinge yard by Plym in 1907 in Honduras mahogany on pasture oak frames, and when we took delivery, every drawer in the dressers and galley still came out as if on roller bearings. For as long as we had her, she remained like that."

9

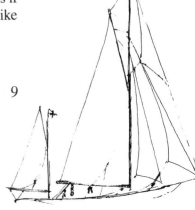

MARISKA

KRATOS

BRASS CABIN PULL

BRONZE HEADSAIL LEAD

Kratos, designed by Albert Andersson, represented the height of east coast skerry cruiser design to maximum dimensions. On the west coast, she was decidedly exotic, a dancer among the brawnier R boats and workmanlike Kosters. The length of her keel, which was short by the standards of her day, made it difficult even to fetch a buoy, Per Carlsson claimed. "She only gave you one chance to do it. Once the short keel lost grip in the water, she took a harbor and a half to start tracking again. But once she moved, she was wonderfully handy and manageable, even for just the family. At sea, she swam like a cork on rough waves. We once sailed over to Denmark, to Skagen, at the northernmost tip of Jutland, towing two dinghies, in four hours—we averaged eight or nine knots. Konrad loved her."

It was a love, however, still tempered by a sober sense of priorities, as a letter he wrote to his married daughter—my mother—in Berlin, on November 3, 1941, shows. "It has been a fine fall. Rutger [one of his seven blockade-running younger brothers] has been home a month, and we have fished for mackerel almost every day. We've had a great time and have managed to salt down half a barrel of fish, a good thing to have when prices are climbing. I have a mind to knot some flatfish nets this winter but cannot get hold of good twine. I've also tried to get some wood, but all dry wood is being swallowed by the war industry. I do have a fine little piece of Honduras though, which would do for a medicine chest.

"They have started building a road to link us with the mainland. I expect that will put an end to our peace here.

"The money is a little better this year. I got 500 kronor ($100) for two months on *Kratos.* I also went with Dahlman for three weeks along the coast on a boat he had chartered."

By the end of World War Two, the grand days of yachting that Konrad had known were fading. He himself was entering his eighties. His joints were getting creaky, and he could not move as quickly as he liked. Yet he never lost his sure touch aboard a sailboat. On the day he sailed *Kratos* from Marstrand to the Långedrag yacht harbor in Göteborg for the last time, an autumn squall was brewing. Konrad was observed by Per Carlsson, who still has a summer house on Marstrand and sails a Norlin 36 with his daughters.

"Konrad came blazing in between the piers without a reef in," Per said, "alone, of course, and with hardly enough room there to turn. He rounded the boat right up in the wind, centered the helm, and began to walk slowly towards the bow. It was agonizing to watch him, as he took one step at a time. When he got there, he just reached out and clipped a carbine clip in his hand neatly to the eye of the buoy, which was five inches away."

The following Christmas, Konrad gave each of his grandchildren a book and a new ten-kronor bill. But a week afterwards, he contracted pneumonia out on the fjord. He ailed for a few days, in his front corner room from which he could see the sea, in bed between the carved ebony chest and the glass and mahogany case that held the two-foot model of *Mariska* he had carved while sailing across the Southern Ocean. We spent those nights in the Marstrand house while mother sat up by the sickbed. One morning she came in, hugged us hard, and said Konrad was dead.

Downstairs, there was a crowd of doctors, clergymen, and undertakers, who were momentarily startled when Jacob, Konrad's fifteen-year-old Sumatra tortoise, crawled out from his hibernation quarters under the bed to see what the fuss was about. We—my brother and cousins and I—were sent out for a walk to stop our guffawing.

A local man hailed us on the waterfront, pointed back to the flag already flying at half-mast, and asked, "Has Konrad passed away then, boys?"

Göran was the first to respond, expressing what we all, oddly enough, would have said.

"No," he said, flatly.

PAID HAND
RUTGERSSON

11

The Folkboat

Besides Dahlman, Mattiesen, and Carlsson, there was in the Swedish shipping business a man called Sven Salén. His perception of life and business patterns was honed to a fine edge in Mattiesen's employ, whereupon he set out for himself, creating the Salén shipping line. On the side, he also managed to be a very competitive 6-Meter yachtsman. By effectively using an overlapping headsail at competitions in Genoa, Italy, he gave such sails their now common name—genoa. He also pioneered the use of spinnakers.

Shortly after the start of World War Two, Salén, as commodore of the Royal Swedish Sailing Society, felt that the time was ripe for a pleasure sailing boat that "ordinary people" could own, sail, and maintain by themselves. The new design was supposed to combine the practical Scandinavian working sailboat tradition with the verve of boats like the Dragon one-designs and the needlelike skerry cruisers.

To find such a boat, Salén announced a design competition in 1941. But as the year waned, no serious contenders appeared. This apparent lack of response became a sore point with Salén, and walking about the Eriksberg shipyard design office in Göteborg one day, he began to grumble about it.

"Strange," he said, "that there is nobody in this seafaring country who can draw a boat!"

As he dropped the remark, Tord Sundén, an engineer and draftsman, looked up from his ship's screw designs. After helping with some 5.5-Meter R boat drawings, he had drawn up a boat according to his own ideas. Gathering his confidence, he spoke to Salén. "Mr. Shipowner," he said timidly, "do you want to look at a boat I have here?"

Salén looked gruffly at the plans the young fellow with sea-blue eyes and high cheekbones drew forward from behind his desk. What he saw was a boat that cut the bulk out of the traditional workboat lines but retained a measure of sober practicality, not the least of which was the inexpensive lapstrake construction. Aft, the

ARENDAL BOATYARD
FEBRUARY 1942
FOLKBOAT 9 1

12

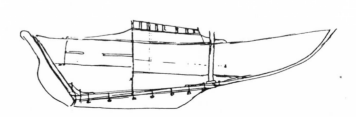

hull was cut off in a rather shocking way, but at an acute angle that complimented the lines in general. He stabbed a finger at the drawing. "This is the folkboat!"

A few weeks later, Salén, as skilled a program manager as Sundén could have desired, had commissioned an initial series of sixty boats. It was a huge number for the time but economically feasible because of the well-established building method.

The first Nordic Folkboats (the official name) were produced in the spring of 1942. A master hull had established the number of hull planks at sixteen, and general building practice was fixed in a set of rules. The wartime hull building material was limited to Swedish pine, with a plank thickness of fourteen millimeters, about one-half inch.

As the project progressed, Sundén found occasion to change some design details. The fully battened mainsail was first to go, in the interest of simplicity. The canvas cot designed to fit in the cockpit found a better place under the foredeck. But the overall concept remained. While the lines sought speed, the gear was simple and workmanlike, easily within a man's strength to handle even in rough weather. Four-part tackles tensioned the jib halyard and jib sheets, with no need for mechanical winches. Everything was trimmed by hand and feel.

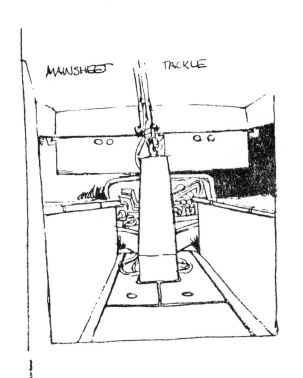

MAINSHEET TACKLE

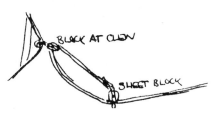

BLOCK AT CLEW

SHEET BLOCK

JIB TACKLE

FOLKBOAT
SAIL CONTROL

The 7/8ths rig had hefty seven-millimeter wire that one could grip handily in the lowers and headstay, coming down to five millimeters in the jumper strut supports and three millimeters in the token backstay. The sturdy Swedish pine mast went through the deck to a step on the keel, but there was the option of an on-deck step with extra back-angled lowers. An almost level floor extended from the cabin into the cockpit, allowing one to saunter in and out on the same level. The deck, being low enough to ship green water, was fenced off with a large coaming. The Folkboat was sailed from the deep, nonself-draining cockpit, with ample shelter for the crew. You could even, as old boatmen like Konrad preferred, stand up and sail.

It was, nevertheless, a radical boat for people used to lapstraked double-enders. Lennart Olsson, who later became chief measurer of the Royal Swedish Sailing Association, was studying shipbuilding at the Chalmers Institute of Technology in Göteborg in 1942 and went out to see the first Folkboats being built. "The hull was incomprehensible at first," he remembered, "the way it had been cut away aft. A boat that size, built on traditional lines, just had to be a Koster double-ender, and the Folkboat was not. It took some time to get used to it." But success for the Folkboat came quickly and convincingly, borne up by a new kind of sailor. For professional men in the city, and many others, it provided at an affordable price a replacement for something they had lost—a bit of weekend freedom at the helm of a sailboat.

The Folkboat prospered, with fleets being formed in many places and individual boats sailing around the world. Sometimes, an extra topside plank was added by builders in Great Britain and Australia and sometimes even a new rig. Colonel "Blondie" Hasler's Folkboat, *Jester,* sparked off the idea of a singlehanded transatlantic race in 1960, by virtue of her seakeeping ability and easily handled junk rig. Hasler took her from Plymouth, England, to Sandy Hook, New Jersey, in forty-odd days, sheeting and reefing the 240-square-foot, through-battened sail almost entirely from the circular hatch with which he had crowned *Jester*'s custom-made superstructure. The unstayed stubby mast needed no shroud tweaking, and an early

14

TORD AND JÖRGEN SUNDÉN
SAILING THE NORDIC FOLKBOAT
OFF MARSTRAND
* 1958 *

version of the wind vane that bears Hasler's name did much of the steering. The Folkboat itself came to be recognized as the small, seaworthy cruiser incarnate. The standard boat was tough, inexpensive, and practical. One person could handle it easily, and it had a smart, built-in performance that did not depend on constant sail-handling.

But although his concept was accepted, Tord Sundén saw no financial reward from the design, even from boats built under the eye of the Royal Swedish Sailing Association. Under Salén's powerful thumb, the association had bought the Folkboat plans outright with the small prize for the original competition. While thousands of Folkboats were being built, the designer was involved in a succes-

15

sion of legal wrangles that ended in an out-of-court settlement in which he was assured of 300 kronor per boat. But by then, the wooden boat market was declining; fiberglass had become the favorite boat material. In 1966, Sundén drew up plans for a modified glass Folkboat. In a hopeful vein, he named the new boat the International Folkboat. In character, it amounts to an entirely new vessel, but the design changes were few, as he once told me. "I kept the hull sections but drew out the bow a bit and rounded off the stern for appearance's sake. To make more room inside, the free-board went up ten centimeters. The lapstrake hull, originally dictated by the wood planking, could be made smooth to reduce wetted surface a little.

"I had to bow to demands for a self-draining cockpit, which is thought to be safer—although I've never heard of a swamped Folkboat. A new rig allowed for the use of overlapping genoas and made room for a decent-sized spinnaker under the higher headstay attachment point."

Sundén's subsequent folk boat designs, such as the Sunwind, retain only the general length and displacement of the original, accepting market demand for standing room and toilet below and a rig needing a fair amount of sail control hardware. The emphasis on sailing qualities, self-reliance, and contact with the elements shifted as the freeboard rose from one foot eight inches to four feet ten inches.

At our last meeting in Marstrand, Sundén spoke about the new breed with a burst of emotion, as *jävla lådor* ("goddamned boxes"). "We live in a strange time, and boats are formed by their time," said the silver-haired designer. "At the boat shows, people climb on board a boat wearing muddy boots and duck below to make sure a twenty-seven-footer has standing headroom everywhere, that she sleeps at least five grown-ups, and that the auxiliary has fifteen or twenty horsepower."

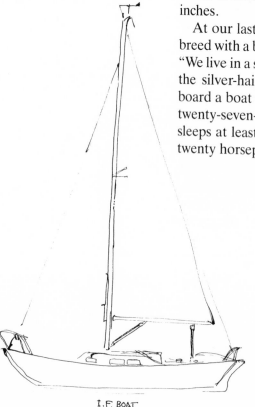

I.F. BOAT

The Marstrand Road Show

Of the kids who grew up on the Marstrand waterfront in the 1950s, Benjy, Lars, Göran, Sven, and I were among the last to learn to sail in eka work boats of local origin, not to mention sailing craft we created ourselves. For our earliest, we begged sugar cartons from the island store and "sailed" them on the gravel path by the lilac arbor. Benjy even cut out and attached a realistic rudder to his carton, along with a primitive spritsail rig.

One winter, when the waters around the island turned into dark green, resilient saltwater ice, we took to ice sailing. We already had ice skates, although they were nothing more than simple, sheet metal cutouts adjusted by a worm gear to fit our winter boots. With a hand from Konrad, Benjy made a hand-held sail from a couple of split dinghy oars and bits of mildewed sailcloth.

My cousin Lars, fearless as always, tried this sail out on clean, wind-swept ice under the old people's home, with the wind from the North Sea blowing at around twenty knots. To our delight, and to the delight of a number of people fishing through holes in the ice, Lars was carried along at a spectacular speed. At first, he was able to remain half-standing; next he was half-sitting; and finally he was lying down, being carried across the harbor to the Marstrand shipyard.

Cheered by this success, Benjy retired to Konrad's woodshed and constructed an ice-sailing yacht from cheap pine two-by-fours. Our ice skates provided the detachable runners. The helmsman was supposed to steer with a pivoting footrest connected to the forward guide skate with galvanized wires. The remains of a lifeboat sail were called into service, and Benjy and Lars dragged the iceboat down to Kilen ("the Wedge"), a wide, shallow bay bordered by the home guard rifle range and the garbage dump and more secluded than the main harbor.

Benjy, his round, freckled face flush with anticipation, crouched into the helmsman's seat and fitted his feet to the steering bar. Lars kicked the bow runner off the wind, and pulling home the sheet, Benjy sped off, his craft swinging wildly from one side to another,

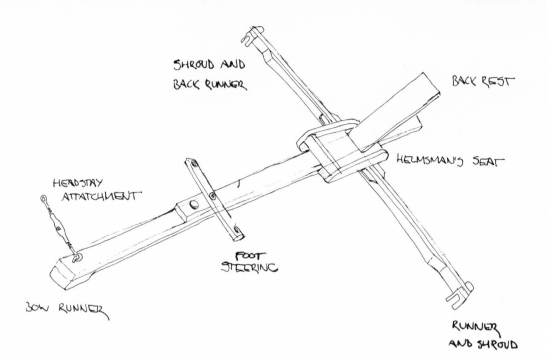

SHROUD AND
BACK RUNNER

BACK REST

HEADSTAY
ATTATCHMENT

HELMSMAN'S SEAT

FOOT
STEERING

BOW RUNNER

RUNNER
AND SHROUD

but moving swiftly. Then we heard the sound of breaking wood; he had crashed. The two-by-fours had not been able to sustain his weight over the bumpy ice. Soon afterwards, Benjy fitted structural reinforcements to the boat, but steering remained a problem with the flat, rather than hollow-ground skates. Lars, taking over a few days later, sped onto a weak patch of ice and was up to his bad ear in ice water before the buoyant, elastic ice bounced him back to safety.

That summer, my family moved inland. My father had returned from a Soviet detention camp and found work in a leathergoods factory in a country village. The village was surrounded by fields, and the nearest stream was five miles away. To pass the time under what seemed a now-suffocating sky, Benjy studied algebra and physics ferociously and built flying model planes of balsa wood.

But as he bent his narrow shoulders over the kitchen table, dissolving celluloid in a bottle of acetone to make glue, we talked of building a hard-chine, plywood cruising boat. It was to be 18 feet long with a swing keel and rudder to allow access to all the islands and bays of the west coast. A small cabin would keep our stores and bedding dry. The sail area was fixed at 172 square feet (10 square meters), and Benjy soon had her down on a set of grease-paper plans.

18

THE ICE YACHT

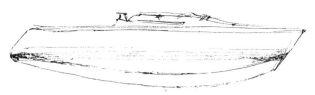

BENJY'S ALL-ROUNDER

In the meantime, with his scholarship funds, Benjy bought a fiberglass Flying Junior—the two-man trainer for the Flying Dutchman. We kept the boat at the end of a cow path, where the sea began some ten miles short of Marstrand. Whenever we could use her, we would pack our fare and bedding in plastic bags and set out, steering north along the coast. Twice we reached the Koster Islands on the Norwegian border, although when we did, our plastic bags were in ribbons and the bedding was soaked through with sea water. But well content in the high atmosphere of the summer solstice, we drifted through the band of pink granite islands, beachcombing and making huge tar and driftwood bonfires at night.

An alternative evening pastime was to sneak into the back of tents where revival meetings were held on the islands. Under the white canvas, we would watch the usually level-headed fishermen flailing their arms, speaking in tongues, and shouting softly to Jesus. Given the time and place, this sudden overflowing of tenderness seemed somehow quite fitting.

In Marstrand, a great change was then under way in the once self-supporting waterside community. A road had been built across the upland meadows and blasted through the rocks, linking the island to a car ferry and causeways to the mainland. The main Göteborg yacht clubs, the Royal Sailing Society (G.K.S.S.) and the Långedrag, introduced their youth training boats—the G.K.S.S. eka and the Långedrag eka. Both these trainers had hull shapes similar to those of the locally built Svennungsson ekas, although they lacked the latter's brave sheer. The main differences were that the G.K.S.S. boat had a bolted-on keel and a sloop rig, while the Långedrag eka kept the traditional sprit rig but introduced a centerboard. It was the Långedrag eka that won out in the Marstrand contest, and for the first time, well-to-do native islanders were persuaded to buy class-controlled sailing boats for their children.

One of Benjy's former school fellows, Göran Andersson, better known as "Maja Cream Nose" (Maja Gräddnos is a self-serving, strong-armed cat in a Swedish children's book), organized Långedrag eka races around permanent buoys in front of the old people's home. He also observed that one of the engineers at the Marstrand shipyard sailed a Finn dinghy, a 15-footer that had been developed out of the Swedish canoe sailing tradition by designer Richard Sarby. In 1956, after quitting school to work in the net-tying works, Göran bought his first strip-planked, canvas-covered Finn.

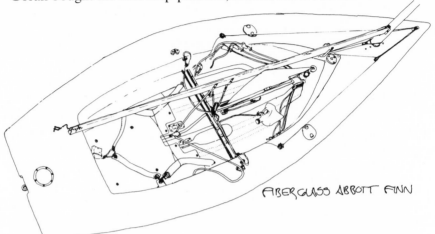

FIBERGLASS ABBOTT FINN

O.K. DINGHY

The net-tying works had an old truck that served no particular purpose on weekends. Soon Göran was carting his old Finn as far afield as Stockholm, the capital. After progressing through several boats made of strip-planked Oregon pine and mahogany, in 1959 he acquired a new Finn hull that had been cold-molded in England by Fairey Marine. It was the first hull to come down to the regulation minimum weight for the boat, 231 pounds, ready to sail. Göran promptly won the Swedish nationals, but took a nose-dive at the Olympics at Naples in 1960, when he had to draw lots for a boat.

Meanwhile, my classmates Leif Enarsson and Sture Andersson (Göran's younger brother) built a dinghy that had been presented as a smaller Finn for home completion in hard-chine plywood. This was the thirteen-foot O.K. designed by the Dane Knud Olsen in 1956. The boats came out nice and sturdy, built from water-absorbent pine ply and weighing in at over 220 pounds rather than the 158-pound minimum. "But we learned quickly," Sture said.

One boat followed another. Göran, who began to sail Finns and

O.K.s in tandem, started to travel widely, stacking as many as three boats on his car. He soon persuaded Fredrik Johansson, a big, florid man who piloted the Marstrand ferry, to start building O.K.s next to the old Svennungsson yard. A fleet of Optimists followed. The slab-sided eleven-footer was rigged with a lace-on sprit sail that marked a sort of halfway stage of development between the eka sprit and a modern Bermudian sail. A talented woodworker named Leif Josefsson was persuaded to build masts.

Göran himself, when in Göteborg, went to the loft of Albrechtsson-Hasse and questioned the sail seaming man, Gunnar Andersson, about how sails were made. He was courteously received and learned the rest by taking apart used sails and noting the cut of the individual panels. Soon he had his own small loft in an abandoned summer hotel. Almost overnight, Marstrand, under Göran's wing, developed into a place in which he and his inner circle could control all the ingredients that went into their boats. He even organized a sponsor for the ever-increasing Marstrand Road Show. The group began to travel under the banner of FESTIS, an awful, sticky-sweet soft drink packaged in pyramid-shaped paper containers.

Despite all this activity, Benjy and I did not join the Show. We preferred our peaceful cruises in the Flying Junior to the regimentation and castelike structure that existed under Sture Andersson's capable management. Each newcomer to the Marstrand Sailing Club was fitted out with an excellent but expensive boat, plus sails and equipment. Not all the would-be champions were successful, but the Andersson loft and related companies, under the name of Marinex Sails, did well.

After winning the O.K. worlds in New Zealand, Göran pioneered the introduction of sail panels cut to Mylar templates to ensure the almost perfect duplication of a successful racing sail. But Marinex Sails were also tailored to their users. Göran's first action with a prospective customer was to put him on a set of scales. A racing dinghy sail had to be built to reflect the weight of the crew, he had speedily recognized, and now, for a fee, he shared his knowledge. The mast, in the boats with an unstayed mast, was as

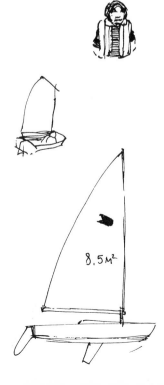

21

important a factor in the equation as the sail. A light youngster required a lighter, more planed off top section to spill air as the mast was bent to leeward in a blow. Göran's in-house mast builder took care to make each spar as required.

The result of all this organization was that Marstrand dinghy sailors, at their peak in a golden decade of the 1960s, dominated the world in boats that, roughly within the class rules, were wide or narrow, shallow or deep-veed. The sail was shallow or deep, according to the helmsman's weight, and it was set on a spar that reflected each individual's style of sailing.

Of my own classmates, two—the diminutive Leif Enarsson and the longer-boned Björn Arnesson—campaigned on the initial Andersson circuit in boats that varied widely in mast section, sail chords, and hull shape. Both took European and world championships in O.K.s within a short time of one another. My cousin Göran, delegated to making clew rings for Marinex after a spell on the Finn circuit, developed the skills to later build up a marine hardware plant on the waterfront. The Andersson-inspired mast builder did likewise.

All this was an obvious change from an era we ourselves had seen, where almost every boat, rig, sail, and fitting was fashioned by the user from locally available materials and commodities such as tar, cordage, and cotton duck. Now things were different. It was at this same time that Benjy decided to leave home to become the youngest of the prematurely stooped theoretical physics students at the Chalmers Institute of Technology. The graphs he drew no longer related to hull lines but evolved into things like satellite attitude controls using onboard computers.

With Benjy gone, I was left to my own devices. I found myself trying to gain a greater perspective on sailing, and one day, I was lucky to come across a letter that Konrad had written on shipboard to my mother from Sydney, Australia, in 1928. "If I were ten years younger," he had written, "I would take you all out to live here. This harbor is a wonderful place for boats."

It was Sydney Harbor, particularly Port Jackson, which linked me even more closely to sailing than Marstrand had.

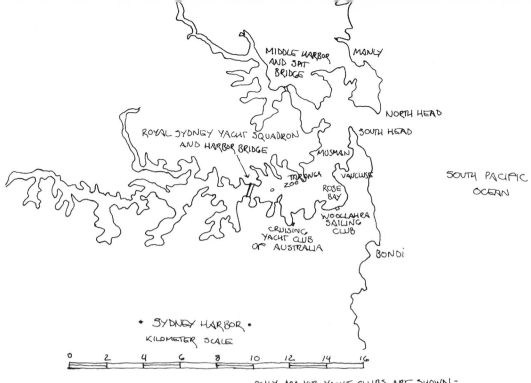

MIDDLE HARBOR AND SPIT BRIDGE

MANLY

NORTH HEAD

SOUTH HEAD

ROYAL SYDNEY YACHT SQUADRON AND HARBOR BRIDGE

MOSMAN

TARONGA ZOO

VAUCLUSE

ROSE BAY

WOOLLAHRA SAILING CLUB

CRUISING YACHT CLUB OF AUSTRALIA

BONDI

SOUTH PACIFIC OCEAN

• SYDNEY HARBOR •

KILOMETER SCALE

0   2   4   6   8   10   12   14   16

ONLY MAJOR YACHT CLUBS ARE SHOWN –
THERE ARE DOZENS MORE ON THE HARBOR

Imperium

When Benjy's plans for his lightweight cruiser fell through and he took himself off to university, I decided to have a look at the small yachts in Sydney Harbor that had so impressed my grandfather. I shipped to Australia in a six-man cabin situated beneath the waterline of the Italian liner *Guglielmo Marconi,* out of Genoa.

I was standing on the liner's top deck, however, on the bright November day in the mid-sixties when she steamed in through the Heads. Before me unfolded a scene even more delightful than any I had previously imagined. In the shelter of the great harbor, with its softly drawn hills and headlands, a hundred different boat types were sailing. The practice of self-reliant sailing and boatbuilding, nurtured by the shelter of Port Jackson, was as old as the original convict settlement. I was lucky to see it in a rich state of individualistic development before mass production boatbuilding killed off most of the classes.

From the *Marconi*'s deck, I was able to watch a dozen races, out

23

THUNDER BIRD
L.O.A. 25'11"
L.W.L. 20'3"
BEAM 7'6"
DRAUGHT 5'
SAIL AREA 308 SQ FT
BALLAST 1,534 LBS
DISPL. 3.650 - 4 -

of individual clubs, all at once. The greyhounds, the 18-footers, streamed up mid-harbor with half a football team on the trapeze. In hot pursuit came a top-heavy green and white harbor ferry chartered for the punters. Ocean racers from the Cruising Yacht Club of Australia were putting out of Rushcutters Bay. The cocky, overcanvassed 12-footers and a staid bunch of Dragons from the Royal Sydney Yacht Squadron sat becalmed near the harbor bridge. Add to this a pair of majestic 12-Meters—*Gretel* and *Dame Pattie,* if memory serves me right—the keen Middle Harbor Thunderbird fleet, and multihulls from 16-foot Quick Cats to full-grown Pivers, and you have some idea of the panorama.

Soon after my arrival, I met an Adler typewriter salesman, Max Crawfoord, who had been the sailing master on the schooner *Astor* and now filled the same position on the 50-foot steel sloop *Bacchus D.,* an Alan Payne design owned by Phil Deaton, a pub owner in Manly, behind North Head. Crawfoord introduced me to Australia in the best possible way, on *Bacchus*'s foredeck.

But my first and instinctive love was for the Australian Moth dinghy, an 11-footer with a highly sophisticated fully-battened sail and a sleek, superlight scow hull that could be built to the owner's requirements. Sailed in the sheltered harbor waters, they were built as flat scows. The Moth was, of course, a far cry from my ideal coastal cruiser, but I found something pretty close to that ideal in the easily built, plywood Thunderbird, of which there were hundreds on the harbor and on nearby Botany Bay. But I preferred the harbor, surely the most wonderful to sail anyplace in the world, to Botany Bay, and in the harbor, the Thunderbird seemed like overkill.

So, between trying to keep away from the deadly clew irons on *Bacchus*'s genoas during tacking maneuvers, I scanned the *Sydney Morning Herald* classifieds in my Burroway Street bedsitter. One day I found, "Moth 355, new Fogg sail, $150," followed by a phone number. The price seemed low enough, considering that the sail alone was worth about half that price, and I called. Moth 355, a snub-nosed, bleached plywood contraption with wooden spars, was sitting jauntily on the front lawn of a white stucco house at

24

Mosman, practically overlooking the harbor. The owner's father, who did the selling, had rigged her up with the spotless new Gary Fogg sail.

The sail set in a perfect arc, with great depth induced by the bottom batten. The rest of the battens, spaced up the sail like so many delicate ribs, were also laced-in hard at the outer end. The

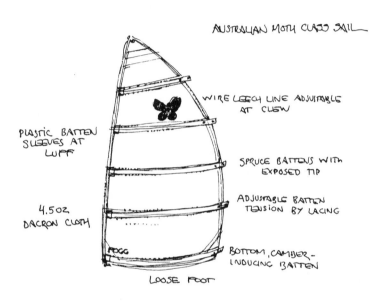

AUSTRALIAN MOTH CLASS SAIL

WIRE LEECH LINE ADJUSTABLE AT CLEW

PLASTIC BATTEN SLEEVES AT LUFF

SPRUCE BATTENS WITH EXPOSED TIP

ADJUSTABLE BATTEN TENSION BY LACING

4.5 OZ DACRON CLOTH

BOTTOM, CAMBER-INDUCING BATTEN

LOOSE FOOT

mainsheet had been hooked on, and the sail, setting on a glued, partially splintered mast and pock-marked boom, wandered restlessly from side to side. I fell for her then and there and humbly accepted the musty smell that greeted me when I lifted the inspection ports, the nails that were working their way out of the bottom, and the wobbly kick-down assembly for the blunt rudder blade.

I brought the boat down to the Mosman spit where a Swedish sea captain of my acquaintance had a waterfront flat. His daughter, a tomboyish young lady with short-cropped, red-blond hair and perfectly proportioned hands, helped me launch and rig her.

"I have never seen anyone look so happy," she declared when I

crawled on board from the crumbling sandstone rocks that served as a landing stage.

My own man at last, on a craft that I could understand and work with, I sheeted home and set my course for the old Rose Bay flying boat base, which housed the Woollahra Sailing Club and a fairly competitive Moth fleet. I could see it just across the harbor, which was just as well because halfway to its welcoming ramp, Moth 355 began to sink. The process had begun earlier, but the water pouring into the hull through numerous empty nail holes and dry cracks took some time to weigh her down. Peeking into one of the inspection ports, I could see water slapping around the inside. Moth 355 made her landfall with the deck awash and the bow partly submerged. For all this, I rather loved her more.

Moth Class numbers by that time were up in the thousands. An attempt had been made to produce the design in fiberglass, but development in the class was so rapid that a mold was rapidly out-of-date. The Woollahra Sailing Club had a fairly competitive fleet, with every Moth representing an individual helmsman/owner who sometimes was her builder as well. The club also had a fleet of Manly Junior trainers (a dinghy much like the Mirror), the fast, two-man Cherub, and a fleet of Quick Cats. All these craft were home-built, hard-chine boats constructed of marine plywood. There were also a few commercially finished Tornado cats in the group.

At first, Moth 355 stayed away from racing, doing instead long, dawn-to-dusk forays up Middle Harbor or sorties beyond the Heads, feeling the deep, long hauls of ocean waves under her diminutive hull and gazing into the blue haze of the Pacific. In squally conditions, her mast shroud fittings used to pull out. Once it happened in front of the 12-footer club in Vaucluse. After drifting in to the beach in front of the clubhouse, we were met by a stocky, dark-browed Yugoslavian club member with his tool kit under one arm.

"You'll need a reamer and prying tool, I expect?" he said courteously.

I was unfamiliar with either but learned quickly enough as he

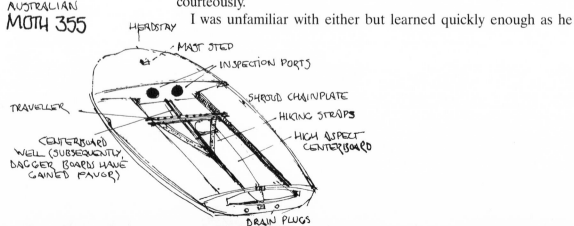

AUSTRALIAN
MOTH 355

HEADSTAY

MAST STEP

INSPECTION PORTS

SHROUD CHAINPLATE

HIKING STRAPS

HIGH ASPECT CENTERBOARD

TRAVELLER

CENTERBOARD WELL (SUBSEQUENTLY DAGGER BOARDS HAVE GAINED FAVOR)

DRAIN PLUGS

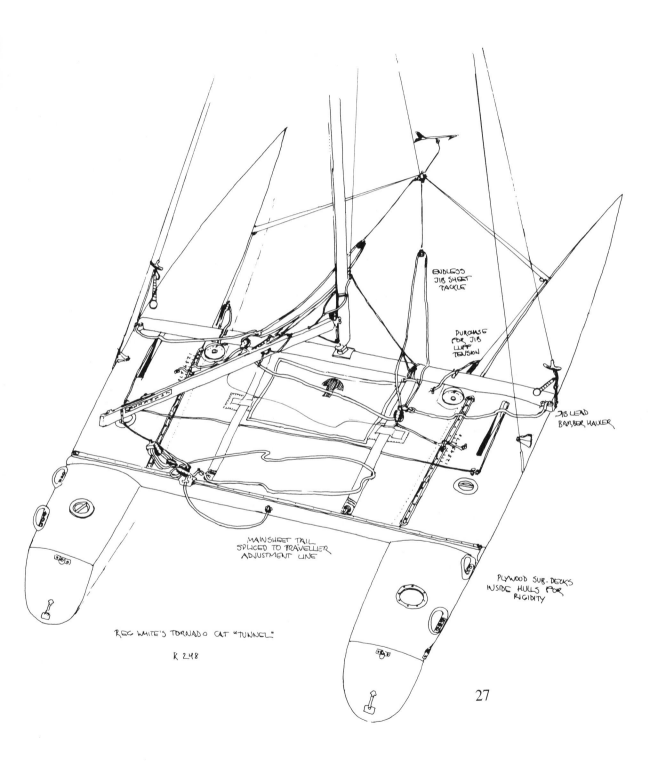

ENDLESS
JIB SHEET
TACKLE

PURCHASE
FOR JIB
LUFF
TENSION

JIB LEAD
BARBER HAULER

MAINSHEET TAIL
SPLICED TO TRAVELLER
ADJUSTMENT LINE

PLYWOOD SUB-DECKS
INSIDE HULLS FOR
RIGIDITY

REG WHITE'S TORNADO CAT "TUNNEL"

K 248

27

deftly reamed open the shroud fitting so it could take a new wood screw, large enough to make use of the enlarged screw hole in the mast. The prying tool was used to make a guiding incision in the mast for the new screw.

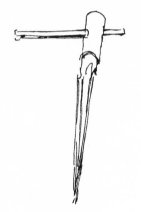

Back on the Woollahra ramp, other fully fledged woodworkers showed me how to plane the pock marks off the mast and how to replace the straight, shedding hull fasteners with screws and ribbed nails that stayed put. On the old club zigzag, I did some sail seaming, feeling as if a thread lost long ago while mending the cotton sail of the eka had been found and picked up.

Neville Olliffe, the wiry club Cherub champion, helped me get one of the coveted inside boat bays, right over the launching ramp. "When is 355 going racing, mate?" he used to insist.

One Sunday morning, she did, when I got caught up in the excitement of a hundred or so people, aged roughly from six to sixty, who were rigging their boats on the club lawn facing Rose Bay and the harbor. As it happened, I was thrown out for rounding the up-harbor buoy but not the tanker moored next to it. My blood was up, however, and I became a regular. Fortunately, the Sunday races were held off a strip of beach where I could go in and stand the still leaky boat on end with the drainage ports open after each race. No matter what I did to her, Moth 355 was at the end of her natural life. In the seasons that followed, I often sailed other more competitive boats, but 355 was my best-loved cruiser, a modest university that I attended and returned to with great joy.

The top level of the Moth Class was a more sophisticated learning institution. Success on the local Woollahra level, satisfying or encouraging as it might be, meant little against the Moth equivalent of the Andersson circus. The boats at this level were fast, light, fragile, homemade shells that commonly weighed in at around only sixty-six pounds. One-eighth-inch Klinki ply was common for the outside shell and parts of the framing. Cedar ply and veneer were used for the transom and for gunwale capping and western red cedar for deck beam laminates and reinforcements. A spruce laminate might provide the backbone, but there was no rigid formula, and everyone built to please himself, always striving to achieve the least possible weight with the aid of various glues, epoxies, and lightweight fasteners where necessary.

Basic cold-molded hulls were available that could be fitted out to individual preference, but the record of successful boats indicated that the boat itself had to be closely linked to the crew. The various black-hulled *Imperium*s belonging to the diminutive David McKay, who topped the Moth elite, are the best examples. McKay made his boats successively wider and lighter each season.

In the 1968 version of *Imperium,* the mast was fashioned from an aluminum mast section sawn off diagonally just over the shroud attachment. Into the hole at the top, Dave had glued a laminated strut that came aft at right angles. This meant the sail had to be square headed, which it was. It was fitted over the mast as a sleeve with holes for the shroud fittings. The individual battens were made from different kinds of wood, according to the desired bending characteristics. The new boat's performance was such that McKay won the all comers singlehanded races on the harbor against champions in larger dinghies such as the Finn and in boats with trapezes.

McKay carried this masterpiece of a boat up and down the Australian coast on the back of a decrepit 1958 Holden. He became a world champion in the International Moth Class as well as in the Australian Moth Class.

"Why don't you try her out?" he asked me one day at Cronulla, his home club. "Just be careful not to put your knee through her." He was not joking, as a couple of deck repair patches indicated.

Nothing in the boat fit me, as everything, from hiking straps to tiller extension, was matched precisely to Dave. But reaching off on a plane over the blustery Gunnamatta Bay chop to Hungry Point, I found the raw power of the matchbox-thin hull and deep-cambered sail absolutely unforgettable.

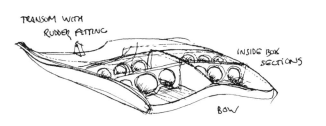

TRANSOM WITH RUDDER FITTING

INSIDE BOX SECTIONS

BOW

AUSTRALIAN MOTH HULL
· UN-DECKED ·

Herr Andersson

As wood gave way to fiberglass in sailboat hulls, the Albrechtsson-Hasse sail loft in Göteborg for a time managed a charmed life, with one foot in Egyptian cotton and one, rather more insecure, in the new-fangled Dacron cloth. From a full employment of fifty people between the world wars, making cotton and linen sails for Kosters and square-riggers alike, the staff had dwindled to five by the close of the 1960s. The principal sailmaker, Engelin, and the hand-seaming man, Herr Andersson, were then in their late sixties and seventies. Sigrid, the seamstress, was not far behind, while Karlsson, the heir designate to Engelin, and I were in our twenties. In Australia, I had come to realize that the joy of sailing was enhanced and mingled with a sense of greater freedom and exploration if you lent a hand in at least some of the factors that came together as a sailing boat. The factor I had chosen, without the least doubt, was sailmaking.

We were called a traditional loft and our customers were men who owned traditional wooden Koster boats. Even when the boats had Dacron sails, the owners ordered cockpit shelters with the light, golden-hued charm of Egyptian cotton. They were men who spent many years wearing out an A-H sail and came back for more of the same durable commodity. But on account of this durability, the lag between visits sometimes amounted to a decade, rather than the year the management would have preferred.

Indeed, our most frequent caller was the managing director of Albrechtsson-Hasse Ship Supplies, accompanied by business contacts from his shipping world. They came to see "genuine craftsmanship." The director would stop at the bench of the hand seamer and say, "This is Herr Andersson, gentlemen, our finest hand-seaming man . . ." Herr Andersson would keep a straight, earnest face and continue to seam away with a swift, economical stitch of great natural elegance. As soon as the audience turned away, his eyes began to twinkle and he winked comically. As the gentlemen left the loft, Karlsson was already reciting, "This is Herr Andersson . . . ," and the subject of our teasing let off his dry, old man's chuckle.

30

And then there were calls from two girls from Göteborg University who were writing a thesis on "Sail Making—A Disappearing Craft?"

To justify the trust a dwindling number of sailors placed in the A-H label, our work methods were thorough enough. When I first came to work under the sparkling blue eyes of Herr Andersson (the title from the director's repeated introductions stuck), he had me making cotton duck seabags from five pieces of canvas to give me hand-seaming practice. A stooped, wiry figure, he spent much of our subsequent hours, days, and months seaming on adjacent benches passing on invaluable advice, mostly by demonstration, and deploring the fact that the *lär-sup* ("teacher's grog"), had been discontinued. In this ancient A-H practice, the apprentice would run down to the corner to get his teacher a grog for every worthwhile wrinkle taught. It was pleasant but idle talk, as Herr Andersson had developed a weak stomach.

Engelin, like Herr Andersson, had grown up at the loft and knew everything there was to know about cotton sails. Already in his sixties and with a reputation to keep up when Dacron cloth made its appearance, Engelin went ahead with a brave face to make synthetic sails exactly as they had been made in cotton.

To minimize bias loads on the sail panels, all our headsails were miter cut. Bolt ropes were unkinked and sewn on by hand and carefully tapered to a neat rat's tail at the end. At the leeches, we cut strips from the panel outlines and carefully reversed and matched them before they were sewn on as leech tapes so that the strains of the cloth pieces would even out. Cringles, rings, and other hardware were worked in by hand, with chafing patches from soft ox-leather sewn on in strategic places.

At first, I found this process rather bewildering, so I put together a paper model of a headsail, with the individual panels bent and finished the way Engelin recommended. (This exercise was akin to the fantastically intricate Japanese art of paper-folding.)

Sigrid, at her ancient Singer zigzag machine, sewed the sail panels together with a double or triple stitch according to the sail's designated use. We all instinctively disliked other hand labor-saving

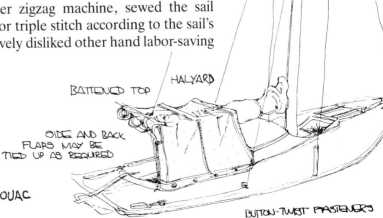

HALYARD

BATTENED TOP

SIDE AND BACK
FLAPS MAY BE
TIED UP AS REQUIRED

HASSE CUSTOMER'S BIVOUAC

BUTTON-TWIST FASTENERS
AROUND COAMING

techniques, such as open-jawed rather than two-eyed piston hanks. It was a matter of seconds to fit the open jaws to a finished sail with a hammer blow or two, but we preferred spending five minutes threading a needle with twine, twisting and waxing it, and then completing the hand-seaming process. We balanced one set of hank lacings against another, feeling in our hands when the balance was

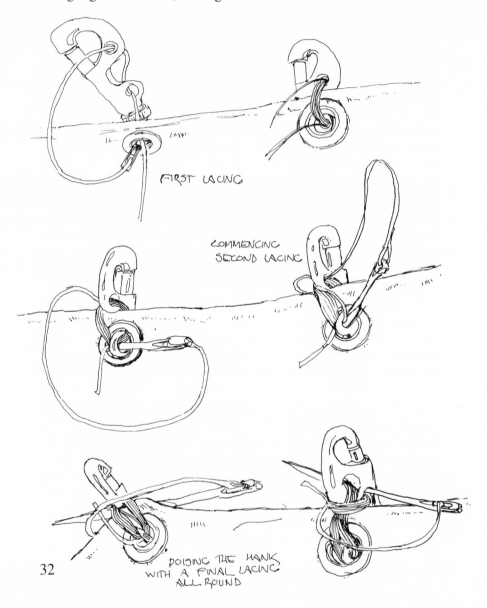

FIRST LACING

COMMENCING
SECOND LACING

POISING THE HANK
WITH A FINAL LACING
ALL ROUND

right and the hank could be fixed in place with a couple of half hitches at the throat of the double lacing.

The making of a full sail, A-H style, was also a delicate balance act. There was the initial cut and overlap (broad seaming) of the panels, the extent of which was marked with the help of long, evenly curved wooden battens. There was the tension of the top sewing machine thread balanced against the bottom one as the panels were sewn together. There was the stretching and unkinking of the mainsail luff rope as it was sewn, stitch by stitch, to the canvas at the penumbra of the contlines of the laid bolt rope. And in a headsail, there was the stretching of the wire or Dacron luff rope to match the tension of the luff itself—before it was fixed in place at either end and with the tightly laced-on hanks. The making of a sail was all a tightrope walk, at the end of which, when your instinct had developed enough, you knew very well if and where you had tripped up the balance.

Herr Andersson showed me these things freely, with a kind of joy in having such good things to demonstrate, *lär-sup* or no *lär-sup*. The only time he got angry was when I once briefly sat down on his workbench to cut a sail seam. A man's bench and his seaming palm, worn to match his backside and the inside of his hand, were sacred things.

For all his mathematical precision in putting in a hand stitch, Herr Andersson did not have much interest in recreational sailing, which seemed to him rather flippant. "Just a great deal of bobbing up and down for no good reason," he would say with a faint twinkle in his eye. "Only time I've ever been out was when Hasse rented an excursion steamer for the staff on May Day, 1923." Herr Andersson, an apprentice sailmaker at the time, claimed that he had had a swell time of it, leaning over the rail, grog in hand, to scrutinize the recreational sailboats for which A-H hardly deigned to make sails, as the profit margin on them was trifling compared to that on awnings and sails for commercial ships. "There we were," Herr Andersson told me on the loft floor some fifty years later, "making a good fifteen knots without spilling the grog, while those little sailboats pitched around like the very devil."

The sails that came out of the A-H loft were on the heavy side, both on account of the detailing and Engelin's tendency to choose a fairly heavy cloth to make sure the material would last out the hand work. But they also had the essential qualities of a hand-made product. If a clew ring or luff wire was damaged, or if the lacings of a

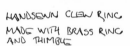

HANDSEWN CLEW RING
MADE WITH BRASS RING
AND THIMBLE

piston hank wore out, it was fairly easy to reach the trouble spot and put things right. A handy owner could, if he took the trouble to observe that the sail was built up by a number of simple hand processes, take it completely apart, by hand, and put it together again.

But one day Karlsson accepted a sail repair that showed how out of touch we were. Commencing work, he rolled the sail out on the floor with distaste. "Look at this!" By A-H standards, the sail was indeed pitiful. A crosscut headsail, the Dacron was lighter than anything we ever used, a number of seams had been ripped out and resewn differently, and hand work was nonexistent. Predictably, the insufficient patch at the clew had ripped at the ring. We all muttered about the casualness of such sailmaking and the new lofts responsible for it. Karlsson said no more about it, but some time later happened to discover that the sail had been in the inventory of the 1969 Half-Ton World Cup winner, *Scampi*. Six months later there was a slump in the semi-trailer tarpaulin business next door that largely financed our sailmaking, and the managing director came around, alone, to tell us that the sail loft was losing too much money, and we would have to look for new berths.

34

Tumlaren

KNUD REIMERS

The attempt to straddle two eras was not confined to the Albrechtsson-Hasse sail loft. Yacht designers of the old school had had to make as great a transition in moving to synthetic materials and new racing rules. A few, such as Olin Stephens and Knud Reimers, managed to place their marks in both the old and the new eras. The influence of Stephens is well documented, but Knud Reimers is less well known.

Reimers's professional saga began in April 1930 when he met Gustaf Estlander in the tap room of a German health spa in the Harz Mountains. Estlander was a naturalized Swede, a yacht designer of legendary skill. In 1892, as a young Finn, he had held world speed-skating records on all distances between 1,500 and 10,000 meters. In 1899, he turned up at a race meeting in Sandhamn in Sweden with *Flamingo,* a racer planked so thinly with pine that he had to cover her with wet sheets between races to prevent her from opening up. But if he drew and built fast boats, he was even more respected as a helmsman. He had a peculiar style of sitting deep down in his yachts—"to feel the boat"—the tiller held lightly over his head, and keeping up a polite conversation with his crew, no matter how the race progressed!

In 1920, he went to Stockholm and continued there as the most audacious designer and helmsman of his day. The boat speed he was able to achieve gained him the name *Trollkarlen* ("the Magician"). The crown jewel of his career was the 15-Square-Meter skerry cruiser *Singoalla,* a lightly built, javelinlike eighty-footer that swept the race courses but leaked profusely and had to be structurally reinforced after each season.

Estlander had long been the hero of Reimers, who as a young Danish student of ship engineering in Bremen, Germany, had been startled by a newspaper story that Estlander was taking the waters at Braunlage in the Harz. "So I borrowed some money, packed my bags with drawings and a bunch of carrots lifted from a market garden, and set out to see him, " Reimers recalled.

Although gravely ill when Reimers saw him, Estlander con-

35

ducted the interview in style. "I placed my previous year's grades on the table before Estlander, all the while mumbling about not having finished my exam," said Reimers. "He swept the lot off the table without giving them a glance. 'Let me see your drawings,' he said. I showed them to him. After a little while, he looked up. *'Wann können Sie anfangen?'* ('When can you begin?')."

Three months after this meeting, Reimers, at twenty-four years of age, joined the Estlander office in Stockholm. Two weeks later, Estlander lost consciousness for the first time and began the battle for his life that ended that November. Reimers had to pitch in, unpaid, to finish the drawings and commissions that littered the office. After his principal's death, Reimers was offered the practice and with a loan was able to buy out the designer's son Tancred.

"When I first filled in for Estlander at a meeting with Swiss financiers and yachtsmen, they looked askance," Reimers recalled. "I suppose they expected even a substitute for the master to be clearly of age." But the Dane had energy and a flair for improvisation. After selling six 22-Meter skerry cruisers to the Detroit Yacht Club for a decent profit, he bought a double-page advertisement in *Yachting* Magazine promoting the skerry cruiser and "Estlander and Reimers, yacht designers" and began to settle his many debts.

Taking the sales angle into his own hands and offering the boatyards a fair profit, Reimers soon had his hands full of skerry cruiser work and even landed prize commissions such as that for the great 75-Meter skerry cruiser *Bacchant*. Her keel was laid at the Plym family's Neglinge yard outside Stockholm, which then was still considered the finest in Scandinavia. Reimers's local reputation spread, although most Swedes had trouble understanding his provincial Danish and, like Estlander, had to venture into German to carry on a conversation with him.

"One time in the fall of 1932, a man called Bengt Kinde came to see me. As I understood it, he wanted a 'modern' Koster boat, longish and narrow, with the speed potential of a skerry cruiser. To make the boat handy, I drew her to twenty-seven feet length overall, and as the lines turned out well, I called her *Tumlaren* ('porpoise')," said Reimers.

36

Among those who saw the *Tumlaren* keel laid was Henry Babson from Chicago, Illinois. Reimers wondered what business the man in the rude suit had in the yard, but found him knowledgeable when they fell into conversation. Their sailing talk continued at the Grand Hotel, where the designer, although again penniless, felt that it would be a civil gesture to buy the overseas visitor a meal. Excusing himself, he went into the men's room and turned his pockets inside out, finding fifty kronor, which just sufficed. "I even ordered in some wine that Plym had told me about. Then I told Babson more about *Tumlaren,* the joy of my heart."

Babson returned to Chicago, and Reimers toiled on in Stockholm. But one morning, a telegram from Brussels arrived, signed by Babson, inviting the designer to present himself at the Savoy in London. "I borrowed money again and went. But at the desk of the Savoy, nobody knew of Babson, or of me. So I wandered about the city all day with a great heartache, thinking, 'Now Knud, you've been had!'"

Making a last try in the evening, Reimers was told that a suite had been reserved for him and was asked if he would breakfast with Babson in the morning. "The next day we toured Windsor Castle with Babson's daughter and talked about *Tumlaren* again. Before he flew back to the States that evening, he paid up for everything, including an extra day for me. I felt like a king!"

MR. BABSON
-IN THE MIND'S EYE

TUMLAREN

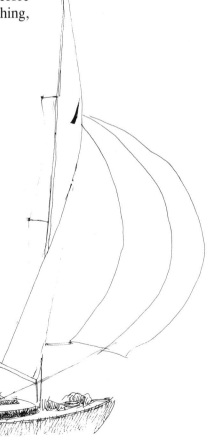

Reimers used the extra day to visit Uffa Fox, the British designer, at Cowes. He found him in the Medina River, on board a ferry. On the flat car deck in the middle, he was building 14-foot racing dinghies, using the ferry's side sections as office and living quarters. Cheered by the example of such thrift and utility, Reimers returned to Stockholm. There, in the course of time, came a drove of telegrams from Chicago, ordering Tumlaren plans.

"I was puzzled," said Reimers, "until I learned that Babson, besides being commodore of the Chicago Yacht Club, was a big man in the automatic milking machine business. And it seems that every time he was about to sign a large contract of any sort, he would put it off to make a pitch that a Tumlaren be included in the deal!"

Although there was not a Babson in every country in the world, the Tumlaren was slowly becoming a world class, and something more. Reimers tried to define it: "At some point in your life you do something, be it a painting, a boat, or whatnot, that touches the heartstrings of people. I did it with the Tumlaren. She was a boat of and by her time, an expression of it . . ."

Uffa Fox, perhaps still under the spell of the Dane's bluff personal charm, called the Tumlaren "the most advanced type of cruiser in the world," while conceding that her concept was unusual and might take a while to catch on, "for it takes years to break the habits and ideas that have grown and become accepted by yachtsmen the world over." But it was only four years after her design that fleets were being established as far away as the Royal St. Kilda Yacht Club on Port Phillip Bay in Australia—with the class rules adjusted locally to allow spotted gum tree for timbers.

The high, narrow mainsail, thrice as long on the mast as on the boom, proved effective and weatherly, seldom needing a reef, and the low displacement of the hull made for sprightly performance. The balance and beauty of the characteristic bow and gracefully rounded stern coined the British usage of "tumlare stern" and related expressions.

Adlard Coles, after owning the Tumlaren *Zara,* had a *stor-Tumlaren* ("big Tumlaren") built. She was the 32-foot *Cohoe,* and

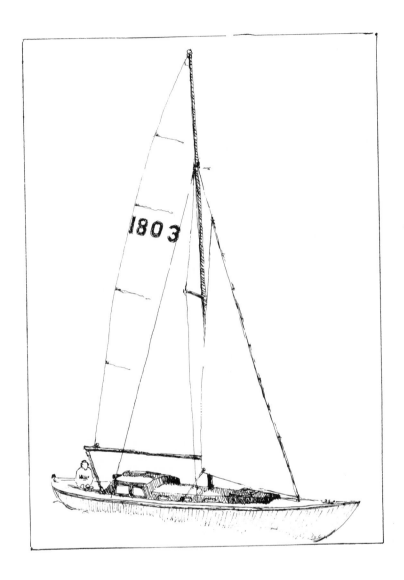

BIG TUMLARE
"JOSEPHINE"

SISTER SHIP
TO "COHOE"

SPLINED HONDURAS MAHOGANY
ON OAK FRAMES
* MAHOGANY PLANKS FULL LENGTH *

L.O.A. 32 FT
BEAM 9 -4-
DRAUGHT 5.6

39

he won the 1950 Transatlantic Race in her. Like those of her smaller sister, *Cohoe*'s design points were a long waterline and a soft tuck to the garboard and aft section that seemed to wipe out the deadening quarter wave of many a meatier double-ender.

Reimers worked on, drawing boats with a high degree of engineering detail. A typical touch on a mahogany eighty-footer that he sold to Giovanni Agnelli of the Italian Fiat concern was a three-bladed propeller that rotated and fed the generator under sail. The same boat pioneered a deck-stepped mast in a maxi-yacht. But the high point of his life probably came when he won the Fastnet Race in his own *Anitra* design.

In 1957, Reimers came up against a new challenge when asked, at the first Swedish boat show, to design a cruiser for fiberglass construction. The 27-foot Fin-gal (a play on Fine Gal) was born. It went into series production in 1961 and showed an astounding turn of speed, though seemingly moderate in all aspects of design. The boat's reputation became such that a plucky teenager called Sven Hellström was prompted to call on Reimers and, on behalf of himself and some friends, ask for a loan of a Fin-gal for racing. Reimers, paying back his own benefactors, consented. "I'll give you my boat and the starting fee; you boys organize your own liquor, tobacco, and girls," he told the rather crest-fallen Sven.

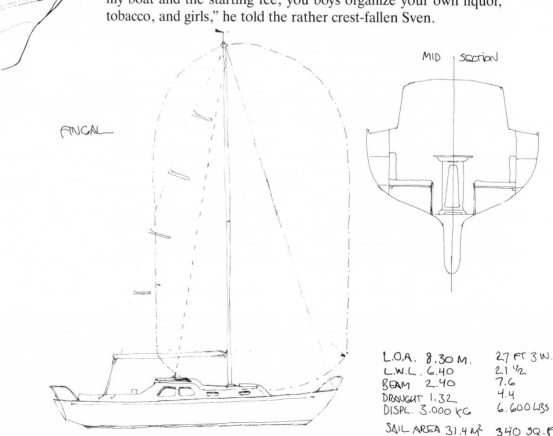

FINGAL

MID SECTION

L.O.A.	8.30 M.	27 FT 3 IN.
L.W.L.	6.40	21 ½
BEAM	2.40	7.6
DROUGHT	1.32	4.4
DISPL.	3.000 KG	6.600 LBS
SAIL AREA	31.4 M²	340 SQ. FT.

Scampi

The pack of teenage sailors who counted the resourceful Sven Hellström as their leader consisted of Bosse Hedensjö, Ragnar Håkansson, Stig Käll, and Peter Norlin. Peter was the runt of the lot, a thin fellow with delicate features and short, blond hair. His favorite reading for some time had been *Nordic Boats,* a coffee-table volume of yachting lore from the time of the swashbuckling Gustaf Estlander.

Norlin's father, an engineer, avidly sailed his 5½-Meter design Nordic Cruiser with his family. His son soon developed the habit of observing the wake of passing sailboats from which he compiled a rough mental classification table on hull drag. Peter himself began sailing at age six when the Nordic Cruiser's dinghy was fitted with a leeboard and a spritsail. In his early teens, sailing a lapstraked centerboarder to the Masunge design at Saltsjöbaden outside Stockholm, he formed his friendships with Hellström and the eventual Fin-gal crew. After their successful race premiere in the fall of 1962, Knud Reimers called the group together. "I am going to supply you with a slightly modified Fin-gal for next year," he said. "The galley has been moved amidships for better weight distribution, and I am going to get some decent sails for you."

In the 1963 Round Gotland Race, the Fin-gal took an early lead in light but persistent air, her crew constantly trimming the new Hood spinnaker Reimers had procured. She soon left the fleet, which included the Wallenberg family's *Refanut* and another maxi-yacht, the Dutch *Stormvogel,* under the horizon. Ragnar Håkansson, a thin-legged Laplander, put himself in charge of sail trim. Upwind, he began to experiment with a new-fangled strop, which he called *prittel-tamp* ("barber hauler"). His aim was to sheet the headsail closer to the centerline of the boat than the genoa track allowed. Stig Käll watched for and called wind shifts. Peter, when he was not on the helm, climbed the mast to see if anyone was coming up from behind. But it was not until they had rounded Gotland and were returning to the Sandhamn finish that two boats, *Refanut* and *Stormvogel,* managed to catch up. The unlikely threesome kept company the rest of the way.

Reimers, having watched part of the race from his Koster, welcomed them at the finish. He was fond enough of all his protégés but had special praise for the second—after Hellström—helmsman: "That boy [meaning Peter] has *fingerspitzengefühl* ('the touch')!"

The Hellström Fin-gal crew went on to win two more consecutive Round Gotland races and take second in the 1968 Half-Ton World Cup at La Rochelle, France, losing only to a fin-keeled Michel Dufour design.

RAGNAR HÅKANSSON
HIKING OUT - STARBOAT STYLE -
ON FINGAL'S WEATHER RAIL
ROUND GOTLAND RACE

The Fin-gal crew had a style of its own from the start. You would never see them at rest on a boat; instead they were ceaselessly bent to sail trim or hiking out in dramatic, acute positions. Sail changes

were timed with Hellström's stop watch, with a perfect change of hanked headsails reckoned to take around twenty-five seconds. Carrying canvas was put at a premium, and they would rather move back a headsail sheet point to twist the sail crazily at the top than accept changing down to a smaller sail. Maximum headsails were ordered in the lightest possible cloth consistent with stretch recovery, with generous deck-sweeping skirts to trap every last zephyr of air. But in the end, as Reimers put it, "The International Offshore Rule killed Fin-gal."

By that time, Peter took an active part in sailmaking. His first projects were small, hand-held ice-skate sail rigs resembling kites, which he made with a heavy-duty zigzag machine bought at a sale;

42

in the spring of 1968 he made his first offshore sail. By then, he had also completed a basic engineering course and landed work in the Stockholm municipal sewerage department. The prospect of drawing up a boat was frightening to him, and he credits *Nordic Boats,* with its rather brutal, down-to-earth stories of design to various rules, with enabling him to go through with it.

"You are afraid when you draw the first boat, afraid that it will not be good enough, that you are presumptuous even to try, knowing as little as you do. It takes a lot of courage to attack a blank design page. But knowing how wildly others had struck out, with success, gave me the push I needed." As Peter could not draw a set of hull lines, Reimers told him it would be just as well, if not better, to carve a model and cut that in slices to get the sections needed for a formal drawing.

In his last summer on a Fin-gal—the year was still 1968—Peter started littering the deck with wood shavings from a four-inch-long half model of an offshore hull. When the sun was high, he would take the model from the back pocket of his blue jeans and hold it at various angles against the light.

"The shape of the hull is brought out by the shadowed portions," he would say when gently questioned about this rite. The model came out short in the stern and knuckle-bowed. Peter explained to his shipmates that the knuckle would stay out of the water and thus reduce wetted surface in smooth water but dip and increase waterline length in a blow. But he left his carefully shaped piece of mahogany behind somewhere in Sandhamn, where he had gone to observe the 5.5-Meter Gold Cup, and it was lost.

The young engineer started afresh, although grieved. Again, a model grew from his hands. This time, he built it complete to one-sixteenth scale, with a Fin-gal model to match against it. "Tank testing" was done in a pond near the Norlin home. The designer measured off the center point on a stick and tied *Scampi* (*scampi fritti* used to be a favorite dish of his) and the Fin-gal to lines off either point. The towing lines were secured slightly off center on the models to simulate sailing leeway. A couple of rubber bands running from the stick to a main towing line secured at the center of

43

the stick dampened oscillations. The testing rig, based on the same principle as the scales of Justitia, was towed behind a flat-bottomed punt.

Scampi always surged ahead. The bow section seemed slow to submerge, but Peter said that slowness could be fixed by moving the engine forward. But there was no easy way of realizing the design, until Stig Käll mentioned that he was looking for a boat. It was quickly agreed that *Scampi* would be built for family sailing, but also for participation in the 1969 Half-Ton Cup at Sandhamn.

From grease-paper plans, *Scampi* was put together in an unused barn outside Stockholm. The high hopes of the builders proved effective enough to overcome the depressing winter winds that howled right through the walls. Dimensions were taken from the lines plan and a set of wooden frames nailed down on the wooden barn floor. These were covered with wooden battens fore and aft, and the mold was turned over and puttied on the inside. After a number of sanding sessions with a tool of Hellström design, the mold was waxed and polished. The glass hull was laid up with a

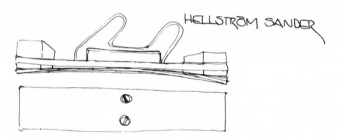

bottom nine millimeters thick, for longitudinal strength, and top-sides six millimeters thick, to save top-hamper. Finally, the deck was glassed on. With summer coming on, the builders cut the necessary hole over the barn door to haul her out, and she was taken behind the farm tractor to the water.

Just before her launching by a Stockholm harbor crane, Peter went behind the customs shed to be spared a possible disaster. But as he leaned, half-sick with dread, against the wall someone came round to say that she floated beautifully. The crew put on some last hardware. There was not enough money for twin spinnaker winches, so a single one was centered on the cockpit coaming aft.

There were also large gaps in the homemade sail inventory, and Peter spent the summer nights leading up to the Half-Ton championships sewing. He knew conditions would be on the light side and put his heart and soul into the maximum headsails. He obtained the lightest serviceable cloth he could get, a three-ounce Dacron with some stretch and good recovery, and sewed it together to maximum dimensions in the simplest, lightest way possible. To twist and open the leech, he cut the customary S-curve into the luff and fitted bang-on piston hanks.

If his hand finish was poor, he was not insensitive to what went on in a sail. Many a night he would slip away to try out a brand new sail in the light breeze on the bay, letting the seams "settle" before trimming the sail in earnest. Peter had rigged a hand-cranked sewing machine on the navigation table and, after observing the amount of flutter at cross-tree level, took the headsail down to bring the leech to flat perfection. His idea was to open two or three alternate leech seams for some ten centimeters and sew them together again, with a twist of his own design to eliminate the tendency to bagging that would disturb air flow off the sail leech. Where the leech was bagging, he tightened the seam; at the leech tape, where it hooked, he eased it. After several of these little operations, with trials in between, the delicate sail stood firm and drawing in any light or medium air, with a perfectly clean leech.

The mainsail, which had mercifully been completed earlier, utilized lessons from the Fin-gal, with Peter adding even more camber and a rock-hard leech for maximum pointing ability. The mast was a small, firmly fixed section in a prototype of what became the Bergström/Ridder double-spreader rig.

The clean, generous sailplan had no excess weight or patching, and the style, with a deep, closing main and well-cambered head-

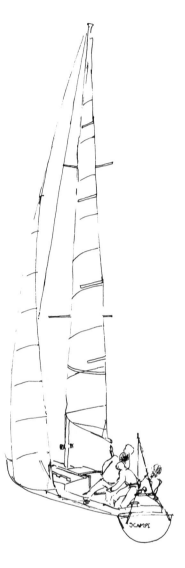

45

sail, sheeted around eight degrees to the centerline and well opened at the leech, was a feature Peter used in his many subsequent Ton Cup wins. But the Norlin profile was never more identifiable, nor more devastatingly efficient, than in the first Scampi.

Ten years later when I saw the boat near the Norwegian border, with a new owner but with her original gear absolutely intact, I experienced something close to shock. The boat was still possessed of undiminished personality, an affirmation of creativity. In his first design, Peter displayed total self-reliance. The working sails were Norlin, the spinnakers (plain, all-white crosscuts) were Norlin, the boat was Norlin, and so was her helmsmanship and sail trim, except that *they* could arguably be called Fin-gal. The main was as rock-hard in the leech as ever, and the light #1 still opened perfectly as she tacked easily through the Havstensund Narrows.

The *Scampi* crew at Sandhamn that first year had the remarkable energy they first displayed on the Fin-gal. Spread over the boat, their wiry bodies were again bent to ceaseless, self-appointed sail trim tasks. Peter himself, over the period of the boat's conception, had become alarmingly sharp-featured and lean, as if he had given of his own flesh to produce it.

In contrast, the sails of the previous year's Half-Ton Cup winner, the Arpege *Safari* designed by Michel Dufour of France, were set on a beefy single-spreader mast section, the genoa had no deck-sweeper ambitions, and the mainsail reef tie-up lines dangled comfortably in permanent rows up the sail.

The *Safari* crew, typifying the rest of the fleet jockeying for Half-Ton starting positions, were leaning back against the weather lifelines in the attitude of men at table after a meal, having drawn back their chairs. Still, as the gun went, a hollow-eyed and queasy Peter at the helm of *Scampi* found himself back-winded in textbook fashion by the *Safari* helmsman. Losing heart in the confused wind shadow of the Frenchman, *Scampi*'s crew was about to make a quick tack to get clear air when it happened. The intuitively built headsail sucked up what confused air there was, and *Scampi* sailed right through *Safari*'s lee.

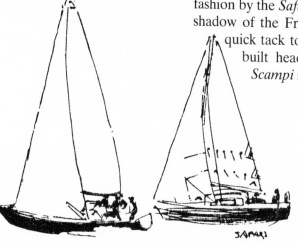

SAFARI

SCAMPI, SANDHAMN 1969

Bris

One summer in the early 1970s, a small centerboarder set out from Sweden's West Coast, her shape giving little quarter to any rating rules or naval architecture. Her name, written in a large, shakey hand on both sides, was *Bris*. Twin lugger sails were set on unstayed masts of the Finn dinghy type. In the tiny steering cabin aft sat Sven Lundin.

There was a rough, unkempt look about Sven that extended to the boat he had designed and built. Simple, homemade fittings took the place of commercial yachting hardware. Sven wanted a free horizon and could conceive of facing it only in a boat of his own conception. Growing up in Göteborg, he was plagued by dyslexia, and because of his general individuality, so easily picked up by schoolfellows, was made fun of for his ways and looks. He began cruising early, in an open eka with a cotton spritsail. Rather than keeping to his native Långedrag harbor and adjacent islands, he started long hauls up the coast, supplied with a water keg and loaves of stale bread.

As one summer followed another, his eka began to reflect its uncommon use. Amidships, Sven built a cubby from scrap plywood and driftwood. It added weight and some top-hamper, but extended with a tarpaulin canopy, it gave some insurance against being swamped offshore. Thus equipped, he crossed the Kattegat one summer and cruised the low-lying Danish islands.

For Sven, much of the pleasure of these low-budget excursions came from the delight with which he and his craft were greeted in some of the "foreign" harbors and landfalls. His fellow cruisers, owners of fiberglass Folkboats, Fin-gals, or other new designs, sometimes laughed at him, comfortable in the superiority of their own craft, but they often stood him a hot meal and some friendly cabin talk at the end of the day.

Back home in Göteborg, Sven began to cut a more outlandish

figure than during his summer cruises. He had conceived a notion that the simplest and most practical form of footwear were wooden elevated sandals of the kind worn by Buddhist monks. Testing out a pair, he would walk around a snowbound Göteborg in blueish, bare feet. With ideas of that sort, obtained from a newfound interest in the public library, he had difficulty in finding a comfortable niche in Göteborg's sober air. For a while, he tried to gain acceptance into a local Hell's Angels group, but his style was too individual. Next, a Volkswagen microbus seemed the answer. But cruising around in that, Sven found the cost of gasoline and professional repairs prohibitive. His thoughts went back to the water as an altogether more realistic escape. His tricks at sea had given him plenty of time to ponder the shape and rig of the penniless man's world cruiser. Sven's benchmark was the eka, and he began to draw an unballasted craft some twenty feet in length. Easily reefed and handled lugger sails of the *Jester* type would be set on twin Finn dinghy masts. A shallow-draft centerboard took the place of a conventional fixed ballast keel.

Making the rounds of plywood yards and paint manufacturers, Sven was able to secure enough discounts and handouts to pull in the materials for his cruiser. He built her himself in the basement of his mother's Långedrag house. The length of the cellar fixed the overall length of *Bris* at just under 20 feet, and the width of the cellar doors effectively held the beam at 5½ feet. His mother had already ruled out fiberglass, "on account of the smell," so *Bris* was built of wood.

On a set of hull sections held together by strip planking, Sven epoxy-glued three diagonal layers of four-millimeter-thick plywood to make a cold-molded hull that was light and strong. On the advice of an engineer at a local paint plant, he painted her with polyurethane varnish diluted 10 percent. Then, before the hull was dry, he followed with fiberglass surface mat painted with the same solution at four-hour intervals until absorption ceased. When this surface had cured, Sven filled hollows and cracks with epoxy filler and a coat of primer before applying the final polyurethane paint. The design was intended for from-the-cabin sailing, but Sven strewed sand on deck before the paint had dried to give a nonskid surface.

Bris's test sail in 1972 took her up the well-beaten path along the west coast, where she could wait out bad weather. Sven was satisfied enough to set out on his great journey in the autumn of that year, after adding 275 pounds of inside ballast. But at sea, even a moderate breeze overpowered his craft and a following one put her into such frightening death rolls that he was glad to reach winter quarters in Amsterdam, Holland. He returned to Sweden the following spring to fit *Bris* with a sloop rig and a 660-pound ballast keel.

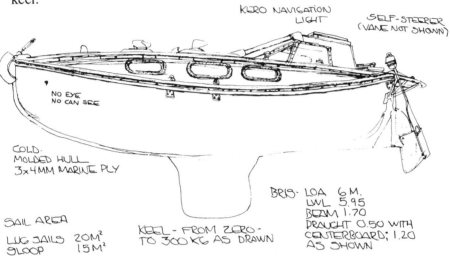

KERO NAVIGATION
LIGHT

SELF-STEERER
(VANE NOT SHOWN)

NO EYE
NO CAN SEE

COLD.
MOLDED HULL
3x4MM MARINE PLY

SAIL AREA

LUG SAILS   20M²
SLOOP   15M²

KEEL - FROM ZERO -
TO 300 KG AS DRAWN

BRIS· LOA 6 M.
LWL 5.95
BEAM 1.70
DRAUGHT 0.50 WITH
CENTERBOARD; 1.20
AS SHOWN

That summer, he test-sailed locally again, and one June night we tied up together in the harbor of Klädesholmen Island, just north of Marstrand. Sven was a coarse-featured fellow with dull, pale skin and deliberate ways, dressed loosely in baggy flannel pants. On land, he moved without animation. But on board *Bris*, he readily demonstrated the finer points of her design and moved without a trace of clumsiness. The layout of the crawl-through hull was planned with a great sense of utility, beginning with a ground tackle pit in the bow. Next came a spacious sleep and relaxation area with shelves for books and navigation gear, lit by a kerosene lamp boosted by a camera flash reflector. Under the bunk there were

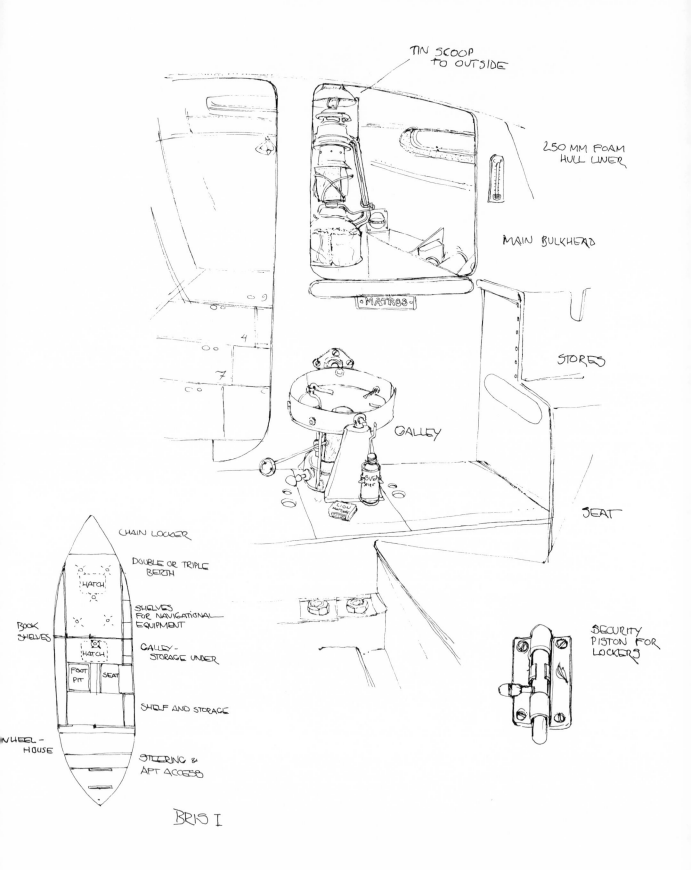

TIN SCOOP
TO OUTSIDE

250 MM FOAM
HULL LINER

MAIN BULKHEAD

· MATROS ·

STORES

GALLEY

SEAT

CHAIN LOCKER

DOUBLE OR TRIPLE
BERTH

SHELVES
FOR NAVIGATIONAL
EQUIPMENT

GALLEY -
STORAGE UNDER

SHELF AND STORAGE

STEERING &
AFT ACCESS

HATCH

HATCH

FOOT
PIT

SEAT

BOOK
SHELVES

WHEEL-
HOUSE

SECURITY
PISTON FOR
LOCKERS

BRIS I

numbered, plywood-covered compartments for long-term stores. Aft of the main bulkhead, below the main hatch, Sven had jigsawed together a galley burner from Svea, Optimum, and Primus kerosene stove parts, resting it in homemade gimbals. Next to it was storage for galley utensils and food, along with an unpadded but comfortable plywood seat.

Right aft, you could pop your head up in the steering cabin while sitting on a storage box. A second kerosene lamp was fixed at eye level for a navigation light. The inside of the hull was lined with Styrofoam packing material for insulation. "I try to make things for myself," Sven said, demonstrating how he had soldered larger tanks to the kerosene lamps.

"Where are you heading with the boat?" I asked.

"Oh, I don't know," he said slowly. "The Pacific, I guess . . . I want to learn about other people, you know. Travel; see and experience things." His simple delivery of these plans was curiously abstract, without the traces of irony, jest, or sadness found in most people's speech.

Sven and I ended up discussing his hand-out Marinex sails—they were flimsy by my still uncompromising Albrechtsson-Hasse standards—before parting ways.

Sven took *Bris* safely to Madeira, off the coast of Morocco, by way of the British Isles. After a rest, he set out for Cape Horn via Gran Canaria in the Canaries. His crew was two women, Dutch and German. As Sven explained it, he picked up the German returning to *Bris* after mailing a letter asking a girlfriend from Amsterdam to join him. From Gran Canaria, *Bris* sailed to Rio de Janeiro, Brazil, and onward south to attempt to round Cape Horn in January 1974.

A message dated August 30, 1974, at St. Helena reached me via the Hasse Ship Supply Office. Sven wrote that the girls had jumped ship along the route and that, "like Captain Bligh," he had had to abandon the Horn rounding and go east, to Tristan da Cunha. "On my way here from Tristan da Cunha (June 15 to July 13), I collided with a whale many times larger than *Bris*. It was a hard knock and pretty scary. I have delivered a mail bag from Tristan, and I might stop here for a couple of months. Then Sweden, or the United

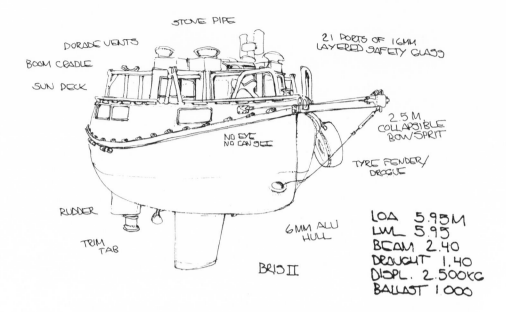

STOVE PIPE

DORADE VENTS

BOOM CRADLE

SUN DECK

21 PORTS OF 16MM LAYERED SAFETY GLASS

2.5M COLLAPSIBLE BOWSPRIT

NO EYE NO CAN SEE

TYRE FENDER/ DROGUE

RUDDER

TRIM TAB

6MM ALU HULL

BRIS II

LOA 5.95M
LWL 5.95
BEAM 2.40
DROUGHT 1.40
DISPL. 2.500KG
BALLAST 1.000

States. With a sailboat you can chart your own course! Sven, S/Y *Bris*."

A year later, Sven and *Bris* wintered on Martha's Vineyard, in the United States. High and dry in the yard, Sven hustled for food money and improved *Bris*'s self-steering. There was an air of home husbandry about his first Atlantic circumnavigation, to which he added by saying he had managed it all at a total cost of around fifty dollars.

Sven's next boat project took him in a curious direction, one that contrasted with his basic lifestyle. *Bris* had been put up for sale, but there was so much of Sven's outlook built into her that buyers to this day walk off dazed by the innumerable Lundin systems on board. Sponsored by the Swedish aluminum spar manufacturer S.A.P.A.,

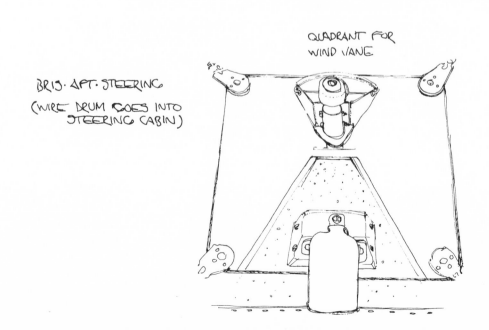

QUADRANT FOR WIND VANE

BRIS · AFT · STEERING

(WIRE DRUM GOES INTO STEERING CABIN)

Sven designed a new boat. It was the same length, twenty feet in length overall. But rather than use the tin kerosene lamp approach, the new *Bris* carried a stereo cassette deck, Brookes & Gatehouse electronics, a Simrod depthsounder, Scanpilot automatic power steering, a Drome radar warning unit, and an Engel refrigerator. Enclosed in the six-millimeter-thick aluminum hull and powered by a ten-horsepower diesel engine, this gear put the final displacement, after provisioning, at 7,716 pounds, against a sailaway 2,650 for the final version of the first *Bris*.

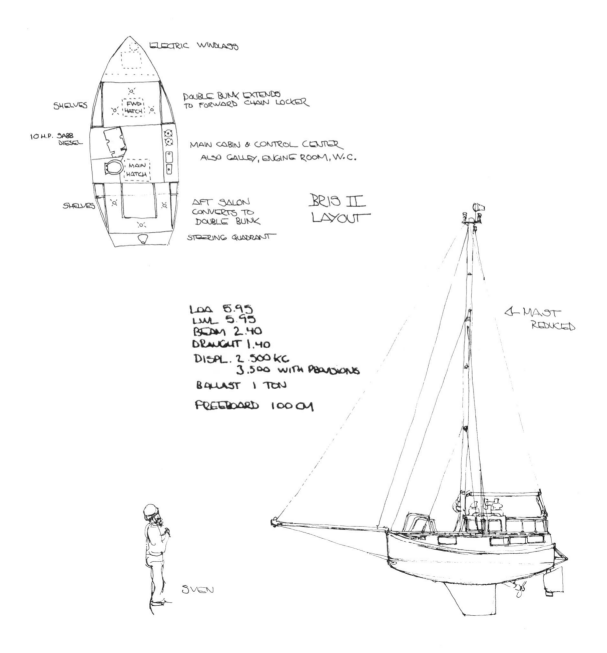

ELECTRIC WINDLASS

SHELVES

FWD HATCH

10 H.P. SABB DIESEL

MAIN HATCH

SHELVES

DOUBLE BUNK EXTENDS
TO FORWARD CHAIN LOCKER

MAIN CABIN & CONTROL CENTER
ALSO GALLEY, ENGINE ROOM, W.C.

AFT SALON
CONVERTS TO
DOUBLE BUNK

STEERING QUADRANT

BRIS II
LAYOUT

LOA 5.95
LWL 5.95
BEAM 2.40
DRAUGHT 1.40
DISPL. 2.500 KG
        3.500 WITH PROVISIONS
BALLAST 1 TON

FREEBOARD 100 CM

MAST
REDUCED

SVEN

The utilization of space inside the hull was exceptional; in lieu of a cockpit, there was an airy aft privateer cabin that comfortably seated five people. There were no back cushions, and a six-footer fit just right. "You don't need back cushions if the backrest is at the right, comfortable angle," Sven observed after the boat had been professionally completed. He was seated in the aft cabin with the diesel oil heater going and a set of binders containing the various instruction books in front of him. He claimed to be bound for San Francisco and advertised for one or two female crew to relieve the chronic loneliness of his way of life.

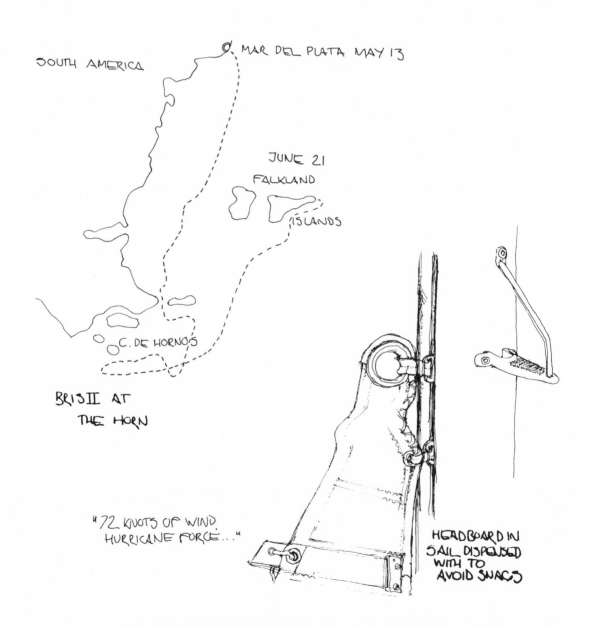

SOUTH AMERICA

MAR DEL PLATA MAY 13

JUNE 21
FALKLAND
ISLANDS

C. DE HORNOS

BRIS II AT
THE HORN

"72 KNOTS OF WIND,
HURRICANE FORCE..."

HEADBOARD IN
SAIL DISPENSED
WITH TO
AVOID SNAGS

At least one lovely set, from France, withdrew after staying for a few days with Sven and seeing the rigging plan. To provide extra sail power to propel the heavy boat, *Bris II* had an eight-foot-long aluminum bowsprit and a towering main spar, all out of proportion to the tiny, short-boomed mainsail.

A trial sail showed that the boat's top-hamper, in combination with the high mast, made *Bris II* excessively tender, and her mast length was cut down by some 6 feet, reducing total possible sail area from 355 square feet to 225 square feet. Sven kept a brave face on it, but one night when we again swung to adjacent moorings, he sketched up a world cruiser of a different sort, a light, aft-cabin ply eka that could be sailed or rowed or fitted with detachable bicycle wheels for overland transport. The sailplan had reverted to a spritsail. "The hull could be hinged on a main bulkhead so you could hitch ocean passages on bigger boats," he said.

For years, I heard or saw no more of Sven. Then, in 1980, another missive arrived, datelined Port Stanley in the Falkland Islands, with a progress report and a map. "My goal of long standing has been reached," he wrote. "On June 16 I sailed alone around Cape Horn. It was blowing very hard, it was dark and cold, and it was very hard to navigate. But the boat is strong and 'stiff like a church,' so she took it pretty well. Will return to Göteborg in easy stages, by-and-by. I have a new boat outlined: trailerable, better insulated (it was freezing cold at Tierra del Fuego, although I slept in two sleeping bags wearing fiber pile overalls and a woolen cap), shallow draft, faster, but almost to the same old length overall.

"Babette jumped off at Mar del Plata and Ilse left at Madeira, so I will try to get hold of a new girl and cruise the Falkland Islands. Plenty of untouched nature here with seals, penguins, and suchlike. Greetings from Sven, *Bris*." In lieu of a sender's address, there was a small drawing of what seemed to be the projected *Bris III*.

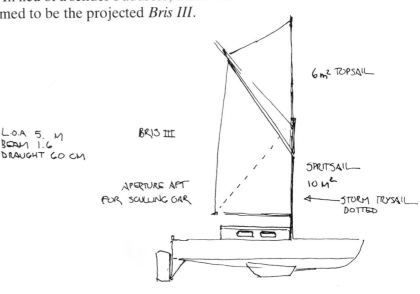

6 m² TOPSAIL

L.O.A 5. M
BEAM 1.6
DRAUGHT 60 CM

BRIS III

APERTURE AFT
FOR SCULLING OAR

SPRITSAIL
10 M²

STORM TRYSAIL
DOTTED

The Colin Archer

My tall, red-haired Coastal Defense Corps comrade Claes Hake grew up on the island of Klädesholmen, just north of Marstrand. Between us lay only the Hake Fjord, the body of water from which Hake's ancestors had taken their family name and which seems still to hold a powerful sway over the family. As a fishing village, Klädesholmen is more pure-bred than its neighbor, with white-painted pine plank houses faded red and waterfront fish processing plants crowding in around a lagoonlike harbor.

The god-fearing and industrious islanders were, in Hake's younger days, supplemented with a solitary artistic summer lodger, who also brought in the first sailing pleasure boat, a twenty-two-foot Cape Cod catboat. Claes, watching the lodger sketch on the rocks, going out in the novel-looking catboat, or just plain getting drunk, was enchanted with such breaches of the island code. The lodger, sensible of his sympathy, paid Claes back with art lessons. As a result, Claes left net fishing one day to attend the Göteborg Valand Academy, from which he was newly graduated when we met in the Corps for compulsory basic training.

On morning parade, the rake-thin, seven-foot Claes was a conspicuously slouchy figure, chewing tobacco and ignoring our diminutive platoon commander, Hamilton. When told to cut his long red locks, he shaved his head and eventually was considered to have such a slackening effect on discipline that he was given an insanity discharge.

Years later, while sailing the west coast, I encountered him often on the Hake Fjord with Bo Olofsson, another son of Klädesholmen but built on a rounder, more florid scale. He worked on marine engine design for Volvo. Mostly, the two were just out for a run, with the one-cylinder diesel turning over slowly and rhythmically—a gaunt, maritime Don Quixote with his squire. More than once, when there was not a ripple of wind on the fjord that bore his name, Claes courteously gave me a tow to Marstrand.

Money was scarce, but when Claes at last received a commission for a major work in fiberglass, he and Bo decided that the time was ripe for the project they had long discussed, a home-built traditional boat of the Redningsskoite and pilot type developed by the Norwegian (of Scottish descent) Colin Archer. Its construction would put to use much that they had learned about work boats as boys on the island. Using fiberglass for the hull, they concluded, would only add to the practicality of the craft. As a kind of pretext for the project, they would discuss the possibility of a circumnavigation under sail.

For a male mold, Claes and Bo put down 100 kronor for a single-masted, oak-on-oak, juniper-plugged Colin Archer original that had sunk at its moorings. The wreck was hauled ashore, turned bottom up, and carefully smoothed. With the aid of some waterfront regulars, they then laid up seventeen alternate layers of fiberglass mat and woven rowing to make a hull that could smash coral reefs and icebergs alike.

The gray and green hull sides of the completed bare hull felt like battlements. But after the deck planks had been added, as in every subsequent phase of the project, there was a sense of logic and

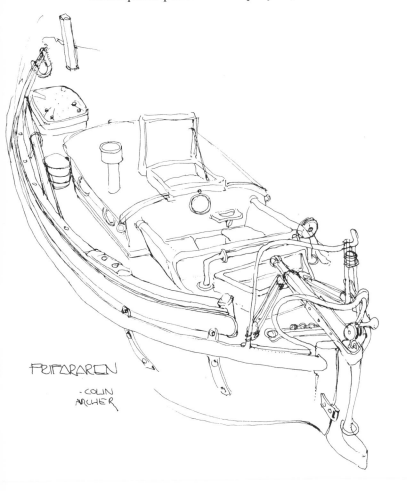

FRIFARAREN

- COLIN ARCHER

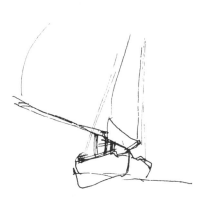

57

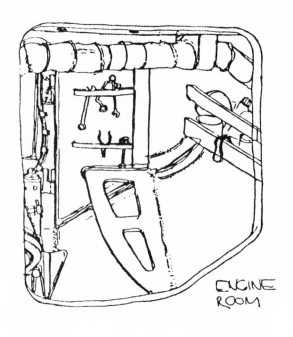

ENGINE
ROOM

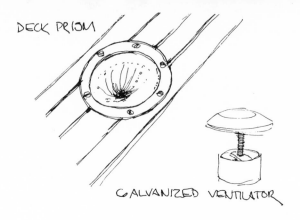

DECK PRISM

GALVANIZED VENTILATOR

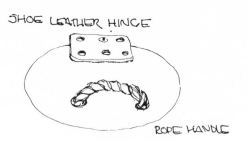

SHOE LEATHER HINGE

ROPE HANDLE

DECK GEAR

utility. Youngwood, an inexpensive but tough wood used as decking in commercial fishing boats, was selected for the heavy deck planks in preference to expensive teak. Other fishing boat gear and simple, strong galvanized fittings were used on deck and in the hand-spliced rigging. Deck hatches were homemade in fiberglass—the gel coat was omitted for better light—in lieu of expensive yachting hatches.

Bo put his engineering craft to good use in restoring an ancient but reliable Scania diesel for auxiliary propulsion. Inside, the sink was given an overhead water tank so that gravity, rather than a mechanical pump, took care of delivery. The seating arrangement for the navigator's station was patterned on that of an artist's donkey painting bench. It was a boat that in every detail spoke of the talents and perhaps even the shortcomings of the men who built her.

58

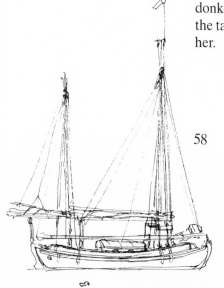

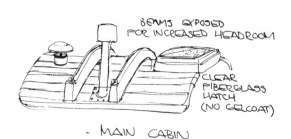

BEAMS EXPOSED
FOR INCREASED HEADROOM

CLEAR
FIBERGLASS
HATCH
(NO GELCOAT)

- MAIN CABIN

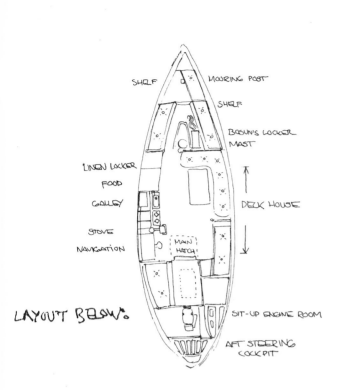

SHELF
MOORING POST
SHELF
BOSUN'S LOCKER
MAST
LINEN LOCKER
FOOD
GALLEY
DECK HOUSE
STOVE
NAVIGATION
MAIN HATCH

LAYOUT BELOW

SIT-UP ENGINE ROOM

AFT STEERING COCKPIT

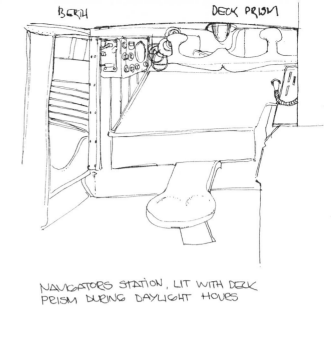

BERTH
DECK PRISM

NAVIGATORS STATION, LIT WITH DECK PRISM DURING DAYLIGHT HOURS

If there was a weak spot in their train of thought, as in the uncomfortably guillotinelike main hatch, it was vastly overridden by the practicality of the sit-down engine room and well-lit (from overhead fisherman deck prisms) interior. Throughout, the builders drew on close and familiar sources. When, after five years of part-time work, the boat was completed at a cost of $6,000, it had in every detail the mark of a sailing workboat. In a summer of coastal cruising, it stood out against the emerging fiberglass cruiser-racers of the Scampi type like black on white.

The boat had no aspiration to be a yacht, nor did it look quite like a work boat, in spite of its lineage. She had a unique quality about her, a something that said she was a necessary link in the lives of her makers. They themselves were as hard to classify, trailing fishing lines often enough and not being adverse to taking a dump over the side, jackknifed out from the shrouds.

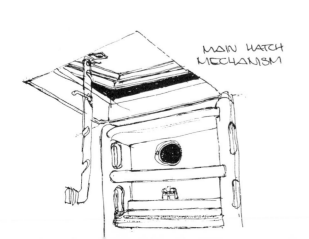

MAIN HATCH MECHANISM

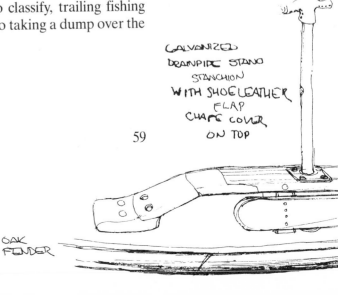

GALVANIZED DRAINPIPE STAND STANCHION WITH SHOE LEATHER FLAP CHAFE COVER ON TOP

OAK FENDER

59

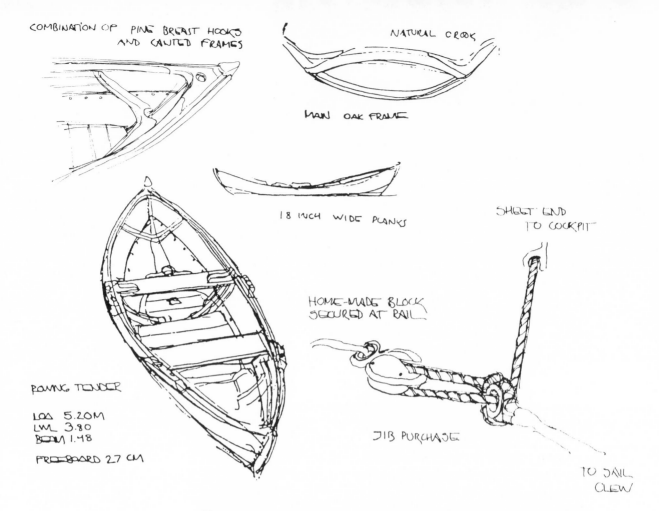

COMBINATION OF PINE BREAST HOOKS AND CANTED FRAMES

NATURAL CROOK

MAIN OAK FRAME

18 INCH WIDE PLANKS

SHEET END TO COCKPIT

HOME-MADE BLOCK SECURED AT RAIL

JIB PURCHASE

TO SAIL CLEW

ROWING TENDER

LOA 5.20M
LWL 3.80
BEAM 1.48

FREEBOARD 27 CM

For a tender, Bo found a wonderfully lithe Norwegian three-boarder. Her poise and narrow waterline made her a delight to row, and for downwind work she could be fitted with a spritsail rig. She was a rare find, as the wide planks needed for her construction are difficult to obtain from an increasingly smaller timber supply.

Claes and Bo set out for Scotland, but at sea the Colin Archer did not quite measure up to their expectation of a world cruiser. The very strength the voyagers had put into hull and rig construction became a detriment. Said Claes, "It was less a matter of being top-heavy than a problem of rigging windage when going to weather. The mizzenmast increased weather helm and windage, so we hardly made any headway in strictly windward work."

The boat, they conceded, had all the rude reliability they had

60

built into it, but sailing was a practical proposition only in winds from a fresh breeze to a gale, and preferably winds blowing in roughly the same direction as that in which the boat was going. In mountainous seas, they would bounce along quite comfortably as long as *Frifararen*, as the boat was named, had a loose rein. Coming off a steep wave, her pinched-in stern threw up such a tail—with water gurgling up to the aft deck coaming—that it acted as a sea drogue trailed astern, slowing them down to a comfortable pace and acting against the possibility of pitchpoling. The hull shape was, in fact, rather close to that of the wooden, 48-foot Marstrand pilot boat: a fine, buoyant seaboat, amply powered and with a vestigial stub mast from which to fly signals. Being realists before anything else, Claes and Bo had the old Scania turning over at marching pace whenever conditions demanded.

Back from Scotland and a scenic tour of the Caledonian Canal, their craft, like many another cruiser on Colin Archer lines, became a bulletproof motorsailer for coastal cruising in her native waters. With her tan main and mizzen up, sometimes to steady her, but mostly just for appearance, and her engine turning over lazily, she became a familiar sight from Marstrand to the Koster Islands. But most of all, she remained a statement of self-reliance in a time of standardization.

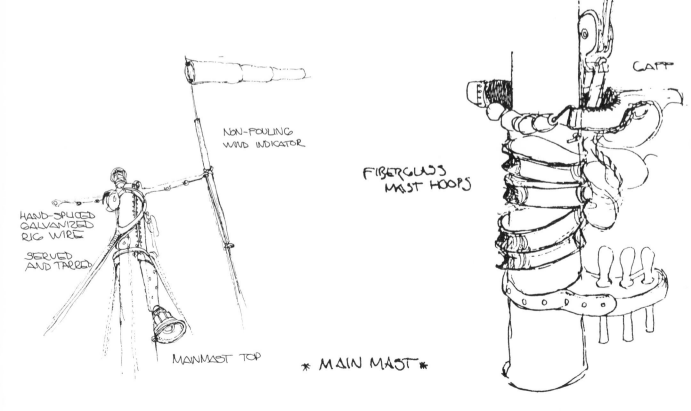

NON-FOULING WIND INDICATOR

HAND-SPLICED GALVANIZED RIG WIRE

SERVED AND TARRED

MAINMAST TOP

* MAIN MAST *

GAFF

FIBERGLASS MAST HOOPS

The Ganbares

Perhaps the biggest International Offshore Rule breakthrough since Norlin's *Scampi* was designed by a jovial, rather cherubic native of San Diego, California, named Douglas Peterson. A onetime furniture stripper who was not at all intimidated by the freedom of a blank piece of paper, Peterson set out to create a rule-rocker, and he succeeded. *Ganbare,* despite a misaligned rudder, was patently faster and pointed better than any One-Tonner of her day. She was launched in 1974.

Ganbare was built, as inexpensively as possible, in the San Diego shop of Carl Eichenlaub, and when word of the boat's success spread, Carl laid on a short production run for people who wanted the latest thing. His name alone stood for something. He was a builder of legendary, race-winning Snipes, other one-designs, and ocean racers and was known for speedy boats in what might be called the Estlander tradition. Two of his Ganbare customers were George Lewis of Sherborn, Massachusetts, and a sailmaker from Chicago named Bob Barton. I happened to be in Boston in 1974 when the Lewis boat was delivered, and I signed on.

Lewis called his boat *Lively.* Her $50,000 hull was built of strip-planked mahogany on laminated oak frames. To ensure water tightness, Carl's work force had covered the hull with fiberglass mat. Lewis spent another $13,000 or so on a sail wardrobe from Hood and yet more money on Stearns-built spars.

Sailing trials were held at Marblehead. Ted Hood and Robbie Doyle came on board and crouched by the headsail tack, looking back towards the leech with approving noises. In her first season, *Lively* won the New York Yacht Club cruise, the Monhegan Island Race, and whatever else could be picked up along the way. Most of the helming was performed, with flashes of inspiration, by George's teenage son, Cameron Carruthers Lewis, better known as Cam.

I left *Lively* to join Bob Barton's boat after it was launched. Bob had made a deal with a Chicago insurance broker named Deane Tank to team up on the boat. Barton was to spec up the boat, make the sails—he then worked at Murphy & Nye—and use her during the One-Ton North American Championships on Tampa Bay, Florida, and in the Southern Ocean Racing Conference (SORC). After that, Tank would become owner, as he actually paid for most of the boat anyway. It was a curious partnership. Barton was a big, driving, one-design racer while Tank was a diminutive, sharp-faced man with kindly, slightly nervous blue eyes.

Barton was not interested in creating a cruiser/racer, nor was he likely to get one from Carl Eichenlaub. The builder's goal was to produce very fast boats in a very short time. *Country Woman* was lofted up with laminated oak frames to which longitudinal mahogany strips were glued and riveted before a layer of fiberglass was laid on. The deck was plywood. Some basic winches were clamped down around the cockpit, a hole was cut for the mast, and some stanchions were set in place. Then it was time to ship her to Clearwater, Florida, where she would be readied for the SORC.

In Florida, the crew did what they could to finish the boat off, concentrating mostly on working up a good bottom finish and generally organizing things. By the time we were done, even the folding propeller blades lined up vertically, with a rubber band holding them to prevent accidental opening. We appeared on the starting line on January 12, facing the ten-leg, thirty-mile, round-the-buoys race in Tampa Bay with the slab reefing lines cut to size and a kedge anchor at the ready to get us off sand banks.

In the light air after the start, we easily cleared Ted Hood's centerboarder *Robin* on the first short-tack—he later went on to win the SORC in that boat—and proceeded to tack to the headers. Deane Tank read the compass headings: "Big header, staying that way . . . tack!"

Country Woman pulled steadily away from the fleet, out-pointing everyone. Barton yawned demonstratively and gave away the helm.

But the walk-over ended with the second race, a 116-mile over-nighter north along the Florida coast to Anclote Key. Moving down Tampa Bay, under the Skyway bridge, and out to sea on the first leg of the second race, Barton again had *Country Woman* among the leaders. It was pitch dark, with a lot of wind and sea building up, when we arrived at the ocean buoy where we were to harden up on

INTERIOR AFT
HAKANSSON-DESIGNED
HALF TONNER
1979

the wind towards Anclote Key. It was essential to carry the spinnaker to the last minute, and I had to get up on the bow pulpit to trip the snapshackle at the clew of the chute. The pulpit immediately collapsed and disappeared from under my feet. As it turned out, only four three-quarter-inch woodscrews had held it down.

Fortunately, another foothold was established, and we hardened up with the crew intact. To free the mainsail leech, Buzz Blackett cranked up the customary backstay pressure. At first, *Country Woman* responded, bashing through the seas fast and vigorously, but suddenly she went slack and lethargic. Bob pumped some more on the hydraulic cylinder: "We've lost backstay pressure!" The whole rig suddenly seemed shaky. Deane Tank looked below and quickly turned back to the cockpit. "There's water coming in, laddies. We'd better pump!" he said.

Stripping off the floorboards, the cause of the geyser coming out at the maststep was apparent enough; the mast had been stepped on the keel, relying on it for a foundation, but the insufficiently bolted keel had been pushed down an inch or two by the mast, producing waterworks through the forward keel bolts. Our handpumps were of a cheap yellow plastic kind, and after ten minuters or so of vigorous pumping to keep us afloat, the valves started to leak and squeak, and after a few hours a pump would be next to useless. Deane Tank cheered us on, indefatigably producing vanilla puddings from aluminum tins, pink and cheerful with excitement.

64

Young Buzz, normally "captain" on the redoubtable Chicago yacht *Dora*, told us while pumping a romantic story of a girl calling him for a date after seeing him and *Dora* on television after the Mackinac race. Dave Gundy, a physician who had shared a berth on the 12-Meter *American Eagle* with Bob, taped a big-bosomed Latin playmate gatefold to the mast. Bob remained at the helm, trying to keep us moving in spite of the shot rig. *Country Woman* made it back to St. Pete in this idyllic fashion, before the pumps wore out completely.

Barton made a phone call. "Yes Carl, she's moving very well, sure; but we have a slight problem . . ." Carl told him it was an easy thing to fix, putting in a couple of tie rods between maststep and deck and between maststep and chainplates. . . .

For the SORC, I handed over my berth aboard *Country Woman* to Ragnar Håkansson, the bow-legged Laplander who had been one of the original *Scampi* crew. By the time he joined *Country Woman*, he had already won the SORC in *Imp* and was a professional IOR juggler, travelling by air to any place in which a wealthy boat owner wanted to obtain the best rating and a sharp crew.

"Every owner wants to make his boat special," he said. "What most of them don't understand is that the process of fairing up a hull and balancing all the other factors against each other begins long before anyone can even set foot on the boat. There has to be a trade-off, too, between speed and other desirable qualities."

Country Woman placed second in her class during the 1974 SORC but by the time Deane Tank took over the boat, as agreed, she was in less than perfect condition. The glass skin was peeling off the topsides and her overall structural integrity was open to doubt. The superiority of her design, however, was never open to doubt. After *Country Woman* was sold, she was refurbished by a new owner and went on to win many races. For Deane Tank, the boat had represented an expensive ride, although he did not seem to mind at the time.

"You come and sail in Chicago," he told me kindly when I left. "We've always got something going on there."

Cannonball

It was Paul Elvström who first realized the idea of an inexpensive, high-performance racing dinghy made by one manufacturer to ensure that all the boats were really alike in hull, rig, and sails. The concept first occurred to him as a youngster when he sailed a keelboat in handicap racing.

"I had very little money, and it was natural to think up a boat that would provide really level, affordable racing for everyone," is how he recalled it. "My aim was to free everyone from the time, waste, and possible acrimony of measurement at regatta sites and to provide a boat that did not need fancy new sails every other month to be competitive. The idea was born like that, not as a commercial concept, with the realization that a truly controlled one-design had to come from one source."

In 1963, he drew up the plans of a singlehander that had been stretched and given a little extra beam to allow an alternative sail-plan for doublehanded sailing as well. Both sailplans were on the generous side, requiring the use of a trapeze in a breeze. The hull was low and rakish, with a negative sheer that cut topside fat to a minimum. My brother, Benjy, and I saw the Trapez prototype at the Göteborg boat show, but being bent on cruising, opted for the higher freeboard and kick-up centerboard of the Flying Junior.

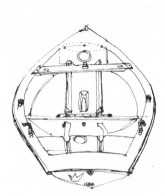

Others must have felt the same way, for sales were slow at first. Hans Fogh, Paul's sailmaking apprentice, told him the Trapez had no future. Still, after a time, the two-man version did start to catch on. In the late sixties, an average of ten boats a week came out of Elvström's works, despite the fact that he had begun to produce innovative Solings and, later, Half-Tonners to his design. "But we lost the Trapez impetus by going into other boats and spread thin our energies," said Carsten Florin, Elvström's boatbuilder. Looking back, Elvström recalled that "the basic idea was right, but the boat might not have been simple enough."

It was left to Ian Bruce, Bruce Kirby, and Hans Fogh (who had by then emigrated to Canada) to pool their talents and create the Laser. Ian Bruce began the project in October 1969 in his capacity as an industrial designer in Montreal. A retail chainstore contacted him to get ideas for outdoor equipment. One item they wanted was a "cartopper" sailboat. Ian delegated the design to Bruce Kirby, who was then editor of *One-Design and Offshore Yachtsman*, a magazine based in Stamford, Connecticut. Kirby, drawing on his experience with what made the International 14 go fast, quickly sketched a low-slung hull just under fourteen feet long. It was at about this time that the retailer decided to drop the "cartopper" sailboat idea, and for a while, the Laser appeared to be going nowhere.

Then, in the summer of 1970, Kirby and his magazine sponsored an "America's Tea Cup" race for boats costing less than $1,000. Ian Bruce built the first Laser for this event, following Kirby's plans. He then engaged Hans Fogh to make the sail and to sail the boat. At the event, held in Wisconsin, the Danish emigré tied for first place.

A year or two after the Tea Cup, George Lewis, a Boston stockbroker, received a call in his State Street office. The caller was a friend of his, Dan Gregory. "Have you heard of these Lasers, George?" Dan asked. "I have been offered a half-dozen of them at a cut price. Do you want to get one yourself?"

George Lewis agreed and presented the boat to his children. For his son Cam, then in his early teens, the boat came as an agreeable surprise. At the North Haven Casino, the sailing club at the family's summer quarters on Maine's Penobscot Bay, Molly Ewing, one of the sailing instructors, had already dubbed Cam "Cannonball" for his energetic sailing in the gaff-rigged North Haven Dinghy. But dominating midget races on Saturday mornings did not represent fulfillment. Cam saw the Laser as a way to open up new horizons.

NORTH HAVEN

The Laser's success in North America was aided by one of the best marketing efforts on behalf of any modern sailboat. By the

67

mid-1970s, that effort spread to Europe, where leading dinghy sailors were enrolled to demonstrate the boat in their home waters. I saw the boat at Marstrand, Kiel, and everywhere else there was a regatta. Then, there were not enough of them to race, just a solitary boat sailing tantalizingly on the harbor's edge. Most likely, it was the same boat every time.

Meanwhile, young Cam Lewis's personal affairs were going badly. He had, in his last year of school, been given the option of being kicked out or doing an outside work project during the last six months. George managed to get him into the Hood sail loft for the work project. Subsequently, Cam devoted his skylarking to the New England Laser circuit, sailing on ponds, bays, lakes, and inlets from Narragansett to Penobscot Bay. He even cut his beer consumption to keep his weight down.

By 1974, when we sailed together on his father's One-Tonner, *Lively,* Cam had become a competitive helmsman, well realizing how much of it was due to his Laser experience. "Forget big boats" was his frequent catch phrase. The family Laser was supplemented with one of his own; the boat's maiden sail was in February and was typical of his emerging sailing style. "It was blowing twenty-five knots out of the southwest. Ted Scott and I cut through the opening in the Padanaram breakwater, coming out on a high tide with a six-pack of beer in the cockpit and stomachs full of whiskey sour 'anti-freeze.' After two hours of high-speed sailing, we headed back on a falling tide with the board humming. The gap in the breakwater looked a lot smaller, but I figured Ted knew the score so I just pulled the board halfway up. Next thing I knew I flew ten feet headfirst through the air before landing in forty-five-degree water. The boat pitchpoled behind me." The new Laser, which had suffered no more than a broken board, was named *The Rock.*

In January 1976, I drove with Cam from New England to Florida for the Southern Ocean Racing Conference. On the roof of Cam's secondhand, red Ford Econoline van were two Lasers, *The Rock* and *Rock II.* The latter, hull 19173, had been added for use in top competition as *The Rock* seemed to have "slackened up" from hard usage. In the back were our gear and some model hulls of ocean racers that Cam had made from bits of wire and solder. One was twenty inches long, detailed with spars and a full sail inventory, including a tri-radial spinnaker with tiny wires representing the seams. The models, unfortunately, perished beneath a trunk during a sudden stop at Wickford, Rhode Island.

On our trip down, Cam asked me to drive whenever there was a good downhill grade, as in the Blue Ridge Mountains in Virginia. He then jumped out with his skateboard, and I would see him in the rearview mirror, gliding from one side of the road to the other. Sometimes I lost sight of him, which usually meant he had taken a spill into a ditch or was holding onto the back of the van.

We sailed the Lasers out of the St. Petersburg and Coral Reef yacht clubs, lacing the dinghy racing with SORC races on the Ron Holland One-Tonner *Silver Apple*. Peter Norlin joined us in

the Laser skirmishes. He finished at the tail end at first, but after some observation, quickly acquired the wriggles and mild body help he needed to place at the top. His concentration was just as good in the One-Tonners, where his own *Agnes,* though considerably slower and pointing lower than the lighter *Apple* in any kind of Gulf Stream chop, would typically be left behind in daylight and then come chugging past, unseen, at night with what must have been perfectly trimmed sails. Much of *Apple*'s best performance was with Cam on the helm, in spite of our distinguished ship's company of Butch Dalrymple-Smith and Harold Cudmore.

The first Laser race proper was the Round Key Biscayne race, arranged by the Key Biscayne Yacht Club. Cam made a late start, capsized, and while bailing out ran into a sand bank at the southern end of the key with the board down. At the main feature of the course, a low bridge connecting Key Biscayne with the next key, he banged into the bridge with his mast before effecting the necessary capsize and dragging his boat under the bridge on end to resume sailing on the other side. Coming up on the last, windward leg to the finish against a stiff breeze, he could lay all his otherwise barely coordinated body energy into hiking out and easily drove past the fleet.

His seeming carelessness was in great contrast to other aspiring Laser champions, like Ed Adams whose singleminded boat preparation we watched during the Laser Mid-Winters on Key Biscayne Bay. Before that series, Cam stayed in the parking lot for as long as possible, drinking beer, smoking a joint, and attempting to fly a forty-cent kite! In fact, nobody in the entire fleet, except locals, was more familiar with Biscayne Bay.

In reality, Cam's *Rock II* had as smooth a board, rudder, and hull as any boat in the fleet, the board and rudder sanded to superb fairness and built up again with many coats of varnish. The boat's stern corners—likely to catch the sheet in a gybe—had been

LEFT SHERBORN, MASS. JAN 17 CRUISIN' DOWN RTE 128

70

carefully eliminated with silver duct tape, a favorite commodity of his in those days. Cam's boat was even equipped with a nickel to tighten up the tiller in the rudder slot. The Fort Lauderdale Laser kingpin, a former Harwich, Massachusetts, biology teacher named Arthur Hurley, was driven to distraction when we came into his beach store one morning and Cam pulled out every new Laser sail in the racks. They all looked very much alike as we held them suspended, but Cam persuaded himself that the seams were more even in one and carried it off.

In the series itself, Cam applied a hard vang and shone in rough air, but in light and medium conditions, his seven-foot height and 175-pound weight were a disadvantage. He seemed to be continually blowing fuses, turtling, and running into things. It was not until the Pan American Championships, some months later in Mexico, that he gained his first prestige win. He arrived for the races two months earlier than his competitors, starved himself down 10 full pounds, and had gained a mastery of both Montezuma's revenge and the local wind shifts by the time the other racers arrived. There was nothing remarkable about his sailing except for the boundless energy he displayed. He moved over the whole trim spectrum, trying anything. His philosophy was opposite to that of the Scot who bought Norlin's third Half-Ton Cup-winning Scampi and promptly taped down every single rig adjustment to lock up the running trim.

It was not until he moved on to the Finn—which he called "a ten-man boat for one guy that makes the Laser seem like a toy"—that he truly met his match. But by then, his Lasers had nurtured a rarely matched skill in competitive sailing. The boats had permitted a gifted sailor to see true progress from one race to another, rather than be confused by the variables one encounters in big boats.

The Elvström dream had come true.

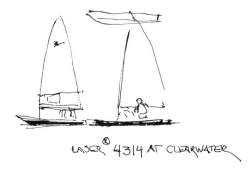

LASER® 4314 AT CLEARWATER

Mattsson's *Chief*

MATTSSON HULL PLUGS

*C*hief, a twenty-seven-foot mahogany-planked one-off, was born when Peter Norlin, the designer, and I called at the waterfront building shed of Karl Mattsson one autumn day. Karl was in his mid-seventies at the time, running one of the few surviving small family yards in a remote part of the Rosslagen archipelago north of Stockholm. His two grown-up sons, Ruben and Josef, helped out according to demand.

The boat we had come to look at was a twenty-three-footer to Peter's plans that was to be produced in fiberglass. Karl was building the wooden plug onto which the female factory mold for the production boat would be glassed. Only instead of building the disposable, simple frame plug that was customary, Karl was building a regular, mahogany-planked boat. It would do very well for a plug, he reckoned, and then someone would be glad to buy the "real" boat, too. His grown-up sons, a little awkward with visitors in their solitary shed on the edge of the sea, looked up from their planes and nodded assent.

The barnlike little shed had a spell-binding quality. I have since seen first-class work in Airex foam, the battens of which were shaped and made to form a sailboat hull with as much care as Karl displayed, but the charm of wood planking is compounded by the feel and fresh scent of the material.

Peter and I had long discussed a Quarter-Ton project. I wanted a boat as fingertip sensitive as *Imperium*. It was to be sleek and spare while built traditionally and strongly from mahogany planks on oak frames. It was an effort to realize my ideal cruiser/racer in a manageable, down-to-earth boat. Peter had obliged by drawing up one we called *Flash*. The rudder and keel looked identical to those on a Scampi, but the relative displacement had been increased and drawn towards the ends a bit.

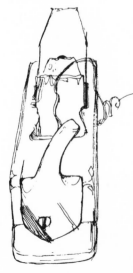

JACK PLANE
BEECH WOOD ON
HORNBEAM

As I had to go abroad at the time, the design evolved, first into a Quarter-Tonner called *Accent*, in which Peter won the worlds, then to *Chief*. The visit to Karl Mattsson was what made building her a reality, prodding Peter to finalize the sketches in 1976. A number of

72

850 KG LEAD KEEL

900 KG LEAD KEEL

"FLASH" 25.9.73
L.O.A. 7.87 METERS
LWL. 6.25   BEAM 2.68
DRAUGHT 1.5

DISPLACEMENT 2 TONS (METRIC)

"ACCENT"
L.O.A. 8.10 METERS
L.WL. 6.30
BEAM 2.70

DISPLACEMENT 2.1 TONS

small improvements could be made from one boat to the other. The keel trailing end was made straight, and the *Accent* rudder that tapered downward was made equally wide all the way down to prevent broaching downwind and improve boat control.

Peter's designs have a dual capacity for speed and load carrying, even if the emphasis is on windward ability rather than on speed on the other points of sailing. A Folkboat, for instance, can be as fast reaching as a fin-keel, spade-rudder Quarter-Tonner of medium to heavy displacement. *Chief*'s size ended up about three feet larger than I had envisaged with *Flash,* but that was all right, seeing that the size, especially with the 7/8ths rig we had chosen, would still be in the right range to allow dinghylike handling.

When I raised the subject of building the boat to Karl, he seemed very pleased. Some time before, he had built the Gotland–Runt winner, a Half-Tonner named *Murena.* "It was 30 feet long," he explained, "same as the shed, almost, so we had trouble squeezing past every time we walked around her." He turned politely and spat out a wad of chewing tobacco.

Chief was built in African mahogany on oak at an agreed price of $7,000 for the finished hull and interior joinery work. No contract was signed. In fact, the subject of signing something never came up, so I don't know if the gentleman's agreement was the rule or the exception. The boat's name was derived from an encounter Cam Lewis and I had with a mechanical Indian chief at Disney World's backlot in Orlando, Florida. Cam made a half-hearted attempt to put him on the van, but even the big Laser sailor had difficulty severing the armored power cord that anchored the chief to his aluminum tepee.

While the Mattsson family nominally worked to Norlin plans,

DECK 2×6MM PLY

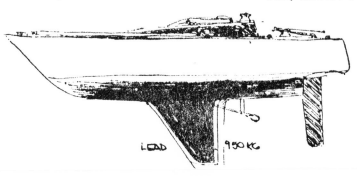

LEAD   950 KG

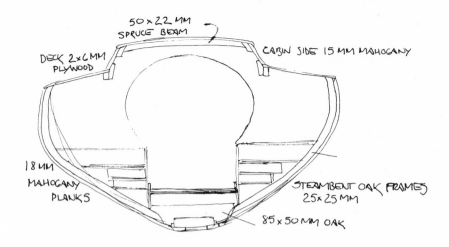

50 x 22 MM
SPRUCE BEAM

DECK 2 x 6 MM
PLYWOOD

CABIN SIDE 15 MM MAHOGANY

18 MM
MAHOGANY
PLANKS

STEAMBENT OAK FRAMES
25 x 25 MM

85 x 50 MM OAK

Karl beefed up most of the dimensions. The mahogany planking, for instance, went up from Peter's twelve millimeters to Karl's stated sixteen, which in reality came closer to eighteen. To support the narrow joint between the National Advisory Committee for Aeronautics (NACA) standard airfoil pattern keel and the hull, Karl added four 2¼-inch by 4¾-inch oak floors to give the keel bolts something more to hold on to than the bottom keel plank (which Peter had specified in mahogany rather than the conventional and heavier oak). Thanks to this, no doubt, and the shock-absorbing lead keel, *Chief* has since survived hitting quite a number of rocks without dislodging the keel or breaking her back. Once, after a particularly bumpy grounding, the forward bolt had to be retightened, but that is all.

With construction underway, I made Peter change the maststep from a masthead rig position to one foreseeing 7/8ths rig and, with moral support from Karl, insisted on a couple of laminated oak frames amidships rather than steam-bent framelets from bow to stern. Karl and his sons, meanwhile, continued their six a.m. to four p.m. working days, finishing the boat in two months. The ingenuity they displayed—making all-wood details like closing locker tops and sliding doors—was remarkable. When I failed to come up with

6MM PLY SLIDER

74

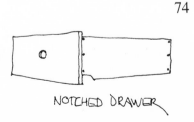

NOTCHED DRAWER

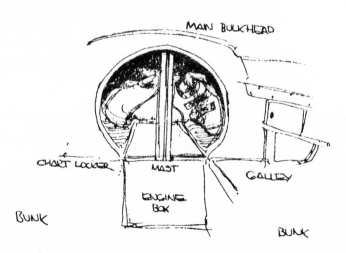

MAIN BULKHEAD

CHART LOCKER

MAST

GALLEY

ENGINE
BOX

BUNK

BUNK

a metal fitting, they contrived a wood substitute. Seeing them at work, making the rather cross-grained mahogany wood yield readily to their intentions, was a wonder.

Their insistence on sticking to woodwork became clear when I made a round of yacht suppliers, trying to come up with a stainless steel pulpit, a mast collar, and four two-inch stainless steel bolts for the propeller shaft support. It was a waste of shoe leather. The mast collar had to be made from a tire inner-tube and the screws countersunk in the kingplank so that shorter, galvanized ones could be used. The pulpit was a reject from the Pelle Petterson factory's conscientious quality control department.

While Karl made quick progress working only with his chosen material, I managed to provide only stop-gaps. The only sources of outside supply that proved entirely satisfactory were one-man-bands like the European Finn champion and mast designer Guy Liljegren. After I had procured a bare aluminum mast section, he designed, made, and fitted the simple and practical rig fittings, bringing everything he needed for the work—and a mongrel dog for company—in the back of his car.

Phil Steggall helped put the sails through at the Hood loft in Marblehead, Massachusetts. There were two maximum headsails, one in 3-ounce and one in 4-ounce Dacron from the Chris Bouzaid loft in New Zealand. The heavier one was cut very flat and scooped out a lot in the leech. A 6-ounce main and a 5½-ounce blaster jib, filling only the foretriangle, made up the rest of the working sails. Three rainbow spinnakers and a blooper were marked up for the downwind locker.

I put the stretchy rope headsail luffs in myself, with piston hanks double-laced, poised to take the wire, as Herr Andersson would have liked them. Cam said a luff groove system would be quicker in sail changes, but in spite of our plans to enter competition I was already looking ahead to cruising. The stretch luff headsails would allow a wide trim range without sacrificing the practical hanks.

My cousin Göran, maker of machine-pressed clew rings that were quickly routing from the market the beautiful, symmetrically sewn rings of Herr Andersson, made the chainplates and a rudder

"HINGES"

LARDER IS ALSO
STEP TO COCKPIT

TWIN SLIDERS
IN GROOVES

STORAGE OVER GALLEY

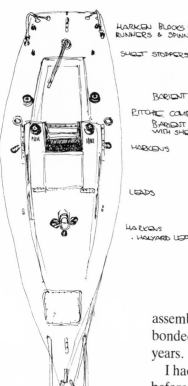

HARKEN BLOCKS FOR
RUNNERS & SPINNAKER SHEETS

SHEET STOPPERS

BARIENT 21's

RITCHIE COMPASSES
BARIENT 16's
WITH SHEET STOPPERS

HARKENS

LEADS

HARKENS
· HALYARD LEADS ·

HALF OUNCE HOOD
SPINNAKER

assembly that incorporated two "ferro-bestos" bearings of epoxy-bonded fiber, which made for tight, accurate rudder feel for many years.

I had really begun to gather equipment for *Chief* in Sydney, long before I knew what kind of boat she would be. A Fico block there, some Samson braid from Boston and Harken blocks from Pee-waukee, Wisconsin—that is how it went. The boat received a weighty liability from a rugged, king-size Bomar hatch I had picked up along with a twin set of heavy Ritchie compasses and a Kenyon log-speedometer set. I had a run-in with Norlin about the Bomar hatch, which he was loath to have installed at a weight-sensitive point in front of the main cabin. Karl, on the other hand, commented favorably on the hatch as being "quite solid."

It was that. Even in a heavy sea, there was no need to lock it down, as the weight of the lid alone kept it watertight. I tangled up the wiring to the Ritchies and the Kenyon hopelessly, but Benjy stopped by one day and fixed it.

From Karl's shed on the Baltic Sea, Cam and I trucked *Chief* down to the Marstrand waterfront, where we worked on the finishing touches in the shadow of the clew ring plant. Karl had readily agreed to dispense with any varnish on the inside of the hull, and I mixed up a fifty-fifty batch of linseed oil and a bug-killer called

Intertox with which I soaked the inside several times over. The Intertox made you choke, and Cam wisely decided to tackle the keel finish—on the outside. He went at it with several casks of auto body filler, long sanding battens, and a marker pen to circle hollows.

Göran Andersson, Björn Arnesson, and the other Marinex/Horizon sailmakers, along with sundry waterfront regulars of the retired Navy officer type, commented appreciatively as he went into his second week of dawn-to-dusk sanding and puttying. There never was such a finely finished keel. The skipper, on the other hand, was reckoned hardly worthy of such a crew, having been known to slip off to some up-island meadow to draw flowers, cows, and other irrelevant stuff.

In truth, when *Chief* was finished, it was in quest of these things rather than silverware that she went. The choice was influenced, perhaps, by her slim, single-spreader mast section's buckling and giving way in the Skaw Race that she entered on completion. Guy Liljegren helped move the fittings to a spare mast section in a day, but the concert piped through the halyard exits in what was left of the mast was not one I longed to hear again. The northern islands with honeysuckle basking in midnight sunshine were calling.

Cruising up the coast, *Chief* is a little compromised by the International Offshore Rule. To bring down wetted surface, the keel area is so small that it won't "bite" at a very low speed. Tacking in a very narrow channel in little air, she loses as much as she gains, eka-style. Of course, under those conditions, she can be sculled forward with the rudder pretty comfortably. But thanks to Peter, Karl and his sons, and Cam, too, I can sail up the coast a boat that has all the charm of the ekas and answers to the slightest change in trim. With just a breath of true wind, she hardens up and proceeds to windward balanced on a sort of knife-edge between wind and water.

She is a boat in which you can go to sleep at night with a faint scent of linseed oil and golden oak frames at your side. By touching the steam-bent oak frame to starboard of my bunk, I can feel the dryness of the hull as the not altogether seasoned frame lifts slightly between rivets in a dry spell. In rainy weather, the strips of teak that Karl used as a substitute for metal sliders for the main hatch jam a little as the mahogany frame swells. She has a hull that, even at rest, makes you listen and observe many things half-forgotten or never experienced.

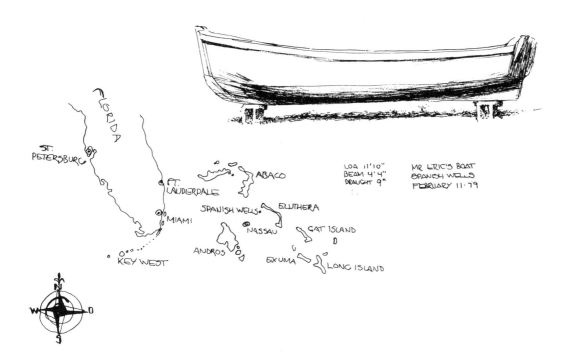

LOA 11'10"
BEAM 4'4"
DRAUGHT 9"

MR ERIC'S BOAT
SPANISH WELLS
FEBRUARY 11·79

Work Boats

The northern fall was not a time to cruise with *Chief*. Every old hand on the Swedish waterfront could, and did, tell me that her clear mahogany topsides had to be under a well-ventilated tarpaulin ashore long before the first night of frost. The porous mahogany, they said, absorbed a lot of moisture and if left there when the frosts came, it would freeze while trapped inside. "All hell will break loose!" was the vivid warning. She would suffer as dire a fate if I took her very far south, they added.

One winter, therefore, I went alone to sail in a kindlier climate. At Fort Lauderdale, Florida, I ran in with Hal and Margaret Roth and spent a night on board *Whisper*. From a stock fiberglass design, a Spencer 35, the boat had been modified in a thousand small ways into an archetype of the conservative long-distance cruiser.

Before leaving for the Bahamas, I sat on top of a chainlink fence and sketched her. Hal came over, showing some concern for how his craft was represented. The clouds on his brow only lifted when

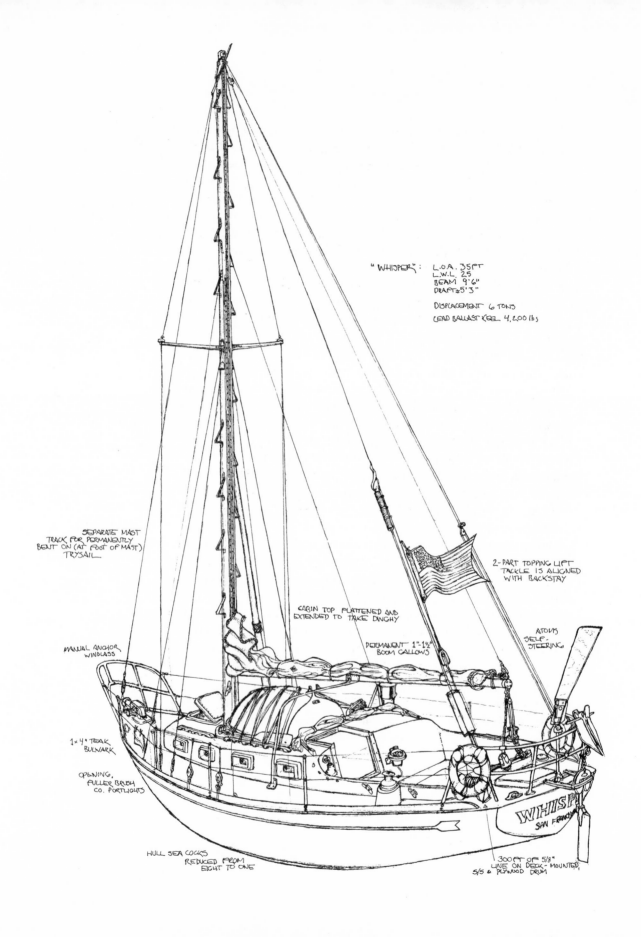

"WHISPER": L.O.A. 35 FT
L.W.L. 25
BEAM 9'6"
DRAFT ± 5'3"

DISPLACEMENT 6 TONS

LEAD BALLAST KEEL 4,200 lbs

SEPARATE MAST
TRACK FOR PERMANENTLY
BENT ON (AT FOOT OF MAST)
TRYSAIL

2-PART TOPPING LIFT
TACKLE IS ALIGNED
WITH BACKSTAY

CABIN TOP FLATTENED AND
EXTENDED TO TAKE DINGHY

ATOMS
SELF-
STEERING

MANUAL ANCHOR
WINDLASS

PERMANENT 1"-1½"
BOOM GALLOWS

1 x 4" TEAK
BULWARK

OPENING,
FULLER BRUSH
CO. PORTLIGHTS

WHISP
SAN FRANC

HULL SEA COCKS
REDUCED FROM
EIGHT TO ONE

300 FT OF 5/8"
LINE ON DECK- MOUNTED,
S/S & PLYWOOD DRUM

Margaret—ever kind and considerate—pronounced the sentence: "That is *Whisper*, all right!"

On St. George's Cay, I met Christian and Mo Kuersteiner, and as they were leaving for a spell in Florida, we came to a happy agreement about my renting their planked waterfront house, "Shellback." With the deal came a Laser that had been dragged up on the weed patch behind the Baptist chapel. This I raced in the lucid green waters inside the Devil's Backbone Reef against Dudley Pinder, a young crayfish diver descended, like most inhabitants in the township of Spanish Wells, from British Loyalists fleeing the new-born United States. Like Göran Andersson in my own Marstrand, he was only the first of a number of people starting to break with the work boat tradition.

It was an idyllic existence, with strong tinges of the island life I had known as a child. Here, too, the language of the island fishermen had its special accent and expressions, and as in Marstrand—where great emphasis was placed on such things as not singing in the morning in order not to cry before night—superstition ran strong. A cough was supposed to be cured by drinking half a glass of salt water on an ebb tide. Miss Mattie Bell at the library— open from twelve to one on Tuesdays, subject to Miss Mattie's gout, which "hurt like the mischief" when the sea wind picked up— warned against standing with your back against the wind as this would cause sinus trouble.

But other remnants of island tradition were fast disappearing. Fishing boats, although still built of wood on Man-O-War Cay and at Hopetown, had evolved, in the smaller range, from the sleek, sailable Abaco dinghy, planked in traditional fashion, to ply or strip-planked glassfiber sheeted, broad-assed speedboats capable of carrying the customary fifty-horsepower Johnson. In the larger, overnight boats, the sail-powered Abaco smack and island sponge schooner type had long since been overtaken by powerful diesel trawlers roughly akin to the Florida shrimpers.

To seek out the remnants of the sailing work boat native to the islands, a type which, according to old Captain Howard of Spanish Wells, had not been seen there for twenty years, I shipped to

81

PEDESTRIAN

SPANISH WELLS

Nassau, on New Providence Island, on the coaster *Spanish Rose*. In the harbor some of the best-looking conch sloops were dry-stored on the waterfront.

The working Bahama sloop, bare-headed or with a jib set on a graceful brace and cutwater, has practically vanished, most having become little more than motorized barges with, perhaps, a cut-off mast and a steadying sail. But some sailing work boats do remain. Out at the Fort Montague Beach, a race was brewing. A brace of sleek-looking work boats swept past, each with half-a-dozen men to windward on hiking planks. One of them shot ahead of the pack.

"What boat is that?" I asked a youngster.

He eyed me with some consternation. "Oh mon, don't you know de fastest boat on de island? Dat is de *Mona Lisa,* mon!"

I soon perched on the outer rampart of the fort, overlooking the bay and the racing workboats *Sea Plague, Kleernaomi, Good News, King of Knights, Mona Lisa, Running Tide*—the individual merits or demerits of which seemed to be the topic of conversation between a thousand or two native spectators.

All the boats were anchored near the starting line, sails down. At a sudden conch blast from the starter's boat, the sails were hoisted on the practically free-standing, broad-based masts, and with an-

"RUNNING TIDE"
BUILT 1976 BY RUPERT KNOWLES
SALT POND
LONG ISLAND

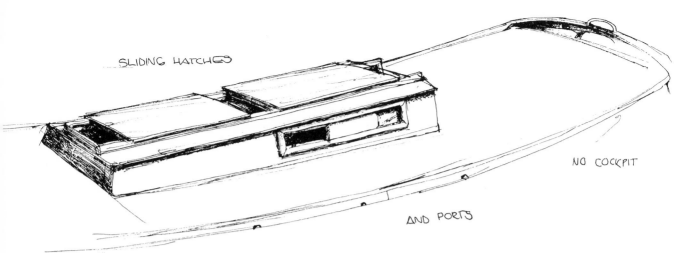

SLIDING HATCHES

NO COCKPIT

AND PORTS

chors still being pulled up by willing hands, the fleet started making surprising time to windward. *Slipaway,* to the intense amusement of the crowd, remained in irons, due to what looked like a fist fight between the afterguard and the crew. Two other entrants, *Sea Plague* and *Good News,* ran into one another, leading to another scuffle. The man next to me, wearing a red baseball cap and with his right hand in a cast, poked me joyfully in the ribs. "Dis is sailing, mon; dese boats don't play around!"

It breezed up, the wind stringing the boats out over the green-and indigo-streaked water between the beach and the first mark. All the spectators were standing up to see who rounded first.

"*Sea Plague* is really going, mon," the baseball cap man said, approvingly.

The crowd cheered when the leaders hove into sight after the last mark of the course, *Mona Lisa* leading the pack to the finish mark, a buoy only forty-odd yards from the beach. She came round cleanly, but *Sea Plague* tossed on her beam ends in gybing, her crew sliding off the hiking plank and landing in the water.

"Bad management, mon," the baseball cap muttered. "I own de *Sea Plague,* mon, and she's winning no prize money."

"She looks like a fast boat; you must get some good fishing out of her."

"Fishing? You crazy, mon? Dem boats are no good for fishing; dey're racing boats, mon, fastest boats in de islands. Dese are expensive boats. De *Plague* is falling apart already 'cause I made them put special citrus-wood deck on for light weight, and it's cracking up, mon."

83

"You're not a fisherman, then?" I said, slowly coming to the realization that I had watched a fleet of *Imperium*s rather than fishing boats.

"Noo, mon. I'm Cassius Moss, former welterweight boxing champion of the Bahamas. Dese boats are owned by lawyers and businessmen, mon. Dey have over 2,000 pounds of lead below,

epoxy-laminated spars, and racks on the sides of de boats for shifting them sandbags."

I returned to Spanish Wells on the *Rose*. On Christian's little transistor radio I heard that the Bahamian sailing authority had decided to allow synthetic sails in the "work boat" regattas at Nassau, Exuma, Andros, Cat Island, and Long Island. Adding to the tide of change, Douglas Brice, a native shipwright arriving from Nassau, told me a new light-displacement boat designed by Charles Morgan for the work boat regatta was building on New Providence, with a finlike vestigial keel.

It was not like the days when, as Captain Howard told me, a building gang might take a couple of dinghies up an Andros Island creek and look for good, full-grown native mahogany, Caribbean pine, or horseflesh, looking in particular for branches and root formations with the curves that could be used for the stem, knees, and frames of the vessel. After some rough hewing, the timbers were ferried to the coastal building site. Often, they were left in salt water to cure against splitting.

The builder would work intuitively, much like the Marstrand eka builder, first laying the keel and setting up the frame, from which

84

grew a vessel native to her birthplace and capable of harvesting its spoils. At launching time, Captain Howard said, a whole community might be down at the launching site, the men passing a bottle around before putting their shoulders to the hull, and with an almighty, continuing shout, push the hull over the sands and into the green water.

It was depressing to see one of the last sailing workboat fleets come to an end, but my spirits buoyed a little one night when one of Garry Hoyt's Freedom 40s rounded up and cast anchor under Pig Island, just across from "Shellback." In her simple (if professionally designed and top-heavy) hull and Hoyt rigging, adaptations of the island-style masts and loose-footed cat sail principle, there seemed to be the promise of some kind of progression for a style of boat that sits so well with her native waters.

A REAL WORKBOAT

cassius moss

Wiåka

O ne summer night, slipping into the dock at Skottarn Island
north of Marstrand, where my cousin Lars runs a boatyard, *Chief* and I had an encounter well suited to put others
in perspective. Inside the granite breakwater, one mooring had
already been taken. A late stroller on the well-planked, broad dock
might have overlooked the occupant completely, seeing how low
she was in the water, had it not been for the canvas top her crew had
mounted over the cockpit. A candle flickering inside the Egyptian
cotton allowed a warm glow to seep into the night and reflect on the
bright curve of the rail around a clean, white deck.

Early next morning, Lars's young son Magnus, Collector of
Harbor Fees, stuck his freckled face down *Chief*'s main hatch.
"Have you seen the little sailing boat that came in last night?" he
demanded. I put a sleepy head abovedecks. In the flat, glossy calm
of morning, the little double-ender sailing canoe in the next berth
rested on the water with supreme assurance, the flow of her hull
lines in no way marred by the pop-up cotton canvas shelter.

I boiled up some coffee, and with that, some buttered rusks, and
a pot of honey, we took up a strategic position on the adjacent dock.
"She looks very easy to manage, doesn't she?" Magnus said. She
did. And there were ingenious touches in her simple gear, such as
the jibsheets crossing over just ahead of the cockpit so you could
sheet in from a windward position.

In the forward hatch, a screw-in dorade vent was fitted, providing

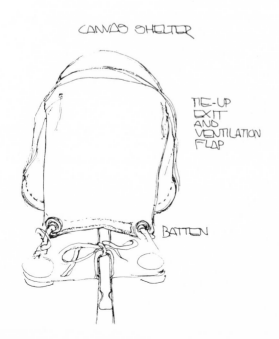

CANVAS SHELTER

TIE-UP
EXIT
AND
VENTILATION
FLAP

BATTEN

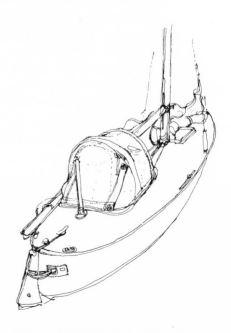

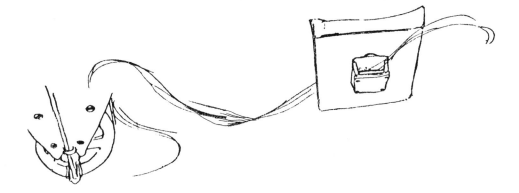

cross-flow ventilation through the whole craft, from the vent to the aft apertures for the steering quadrant cables.

After a while, Magnus cleared his throat and said, "I wonder if there is anyone inside?"

The canoe wriggled a little, as if someone had sat up inside the canvas top. "Yes, there is someone inside," came a polite voice, "and good morning to you both."

After some more wriggling, a tanned old chap in a clean khaki shirt and slacks smartly pulled up the flap at the aft end of the canvas top. His movements around the boat were quick and perfectly balanced. Sensing our interest in the craft, he felt obliged to demonstrate the finer points.

"There is plenty of room inside with the shelter up. You can warm her up in the evening with just a candle inside. The duck top absorbs moisture from the inside and conveys it outside, so there is no problem with damp. And when it rains, the natural fibers swell a little and become waterproof, so you are snug and dry inside. My name is Bengt, by the way." After Bengt had fired up some tea on his spirit burner and joined us on the dock, we found out more. It was his thirty-third cruising season in the boat, a D-class canoe he had bought secondhand in the forties. Mostly, he had sailed alone. "In my younger days, I persuaded a girl to sail with me, twelve times exactly. But she never could get used to tacking, and I always had to do the dishes. Finally, I told her how I wanted things to be on board, and she went home to think about it. Afterwards, she called up a few times to ask if I was still being difficult. But I have had a grand time of it!

"Sometimes, I think the pleasure of sailing and cruising is wholly dependent on how big a boat you think you need. It is easy to say, 'We have to have an engine.' But as soon as you say that, you

SWIVEL
BOW-
FITTING

DECK LEAD

determine many things about the weight and nature of your boat. You may suddenly need a big sailplan, heavy winches, and a lot of other equipment. In this boat, every wave lifts you up and changes the horizon."

Magnus paid rapt attention. It was obvious that he had forgotten about the harbor fee.

Bengt continued, "I am met like an old friend in my ports of call along the coast. It makes me feel like a messenger of summer when people hail *Wiåka* and ask me to tie up at their dock. People have shown me much kindness."

Bengt opened the ship's log, taken from one of the roomy cockpit drawers. On one page was a little poem dedicated to the proprietress of the Lunne Bay Pension. When Bengt blew into the pension's dock at the height of a rainstorm, she had taken him in for a hot bath and meal, refusing any payment.

On another page, for June 22, when the midnight sun gleams on the horizon all night, it said: "Weather Isles, the last outpost of the Swedish coast on the North Sea. Swam at night in the green phosphorescent sea. Picked orchids and a bunch of splendid sea campion. There is honeysuckle here and the scent of centuries-old hawthorne bushes. A small Hawaii!"

Time came for *Wiåka* to press on. There was no wind in the harbor, but Bengt made the eastern entrance with a few paddle-strokes. Outside the breakwater, *Wiåka* met the morning breeze, and the small hull rose eagerly to the lazy swell from the Skagerrak. Bengt carefully trimmed the flat-cut sails and settled down forward in the cockpit to immerse the hull to its full sailing lines. Magnus waved to him and then watched without a word until a rocky promontory hid *Wiåka*'s sails from view.

88

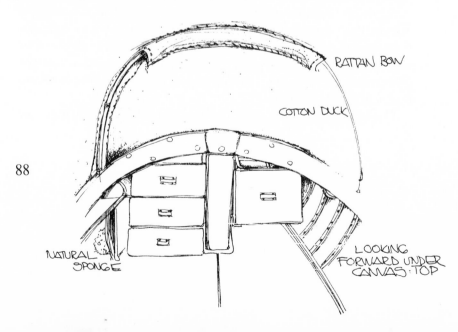

RATTAN BOW

COTTON DUCK

NATURAL SPONGE

LOOKING FORWARD UNDER CANVAS·TOP

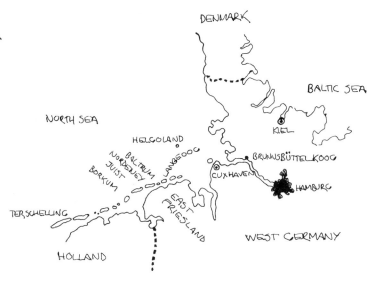

A Kind of Freedom

We came very close to missing the sands altogether. When *Chief*, southbound from her native coast, emerged from the Nord-Ostzee-Kanal at Brunnsbüttelkoog after a rainy night, the swift-moving flood tide in the Elbe estuary seemed to call for an outside passage. A heavy mist enveloped Cuxhaven as we crept past, bucking the current, our eight-horsepower engine struggling at maximum revolutions. The green ocean buoys, laid out like a string of three-ton pearls past the Neuwerk and Scharhörn shoals, tugged at their moorings half submerged, trailing a cable-length of froth to leeward.

In our path to Terschelling, Holland, lay the treacherous shoals of East Friesland, endlessly shifting sands with depths changing continually with the race of the tides. Autumnal gales were in the offing from the Bay of Biscay to the German Bight.

"Let's go out to Helgoland and then lay a course directly to Terschelling," Lisa suggested. She had been dipping into Watkins's *Coastwise Navigation* ever since I went right by Anholt Island on another foggy day, outbound from Marstrand. I agreed, thankfully laying aside the complex, blue volume of tide tables, *Nordzeehoch-undniedrigwasserzeittafeln.*

The fog was burning off as the September sun rose higher, and

89

the tide we were fighting gradually began to turn, sweeping *Chief* seaward to the island of Helgoland at a smart rate, although the engine had been turned off and our sails barely filled in a gentle seabreeze.

Chief, now a few years beyond her conception, had changed a little in concept and appearance as much of the fine brand-name equipment and the Hood blooper, floater, and flanker spinnakers had gradually been sold off to finance my coastal cruising. The working sails were still washed, folded, and cared for in exemplary fashion, the sheets kept rinsed and supple, and the bottom kept clean, but there is no denying that a couple of hull plugs had blackened and had not been replaced. The clear varnish on the sheer was worn and scruffed, and the cool white decks were down to the gray primer in places. With time, I had come to act only on her symptoms that spoke true and serious, rather than bother with things of little substance. The keelbolts were routinely checked and tightened when temperature or season seemed to call for it, and varnish was applied only when underlying wood suffered. My aim was for a balance, a state of equilibrium in which the inward workings were more important than outward appearance. The front end of the beautifully finished lead NACA airfoil keel was full of grievous bites from underwater rocks.

Even the engine had nearly gone after a cash offer on the Marstrand waterfront. I had rarely used it, and the light evenings of the Scandinavian summer had hardly warranted it for charging batteries. A round-wick kerosene lamp provided all the light and warmth needed, especially as the wooden hull was a wonderful insulator, with never a drop of condensation. It was lucky for the Nord-Ostzee-Kanal passage, and for what shortly lay ahead, that the engine had stayed in, but it vibrated like a scared sheep and its presence flawed the boat's natural symmetry.

We gazed into the haze of the horizon and just after midday were rewarded. The vast concrete harbor basin that nestles under the crumbling red chalk cliffs of the former Imperial and Third Reich naval *Stutzpunkt,* or "base," covers a square mile or two, but being tidal and without any facilities for small boats, it does not provide a comfortable mooring. After circling dubiously under main alone along the endless ramparts, we moored alongside an Elvström 32 that had lines to the harbor wall, fifty yards up, and ladder access to the concrete brink.

It was the skipper of the Elvström, a dapper, deeply suntanned man who steered us in the direction of the sands off the East Frisian Islands. Herr Rembert van Delden courteously informed us that he would be leaving early the following morning to reach Bensersiel, on the West German coast, on the morning tide. I told him we would probably start for Terschelling at a similar time.

"Terschelling!" he said. "You are not seeing *die Watten* of East Friesland!" No, we said, claiming time pressure. "Bensersiel is on the mainland, but you must see the islands and *die Watten,*" counseled van Delden, paying no heed to our excuse. "We are sailing via Langeoog Island; all you have to do is follow."

We gave in, in the end. Van Delden gravely promised to bring us over the vast sandbar shielding the islands at exactly the right time. To my occasional grief, I'm a pushover for navigational assistance. *Die Watten,* the no-man's-land between tides, held out no particular promise.

Twenty-four hours later we bore down on the sun-lit ocean beach at Langeoog, slipped through a break in the partly exposed sandbar outside it, and rounded the island along an invisible tide channel indicated by what van Delden called "pricks." They were young saplings, stuck in along the bank to mark the tide channel and the harbor approach between Westeriff and Robbenplate.

The island was a lush green, like a fertile cow pasture cut from the mainland and planted in the blue sea. It stood against a backdrop of gunpowder-gray fog on the horizon, an ever-present circle of darkness in spite of continually sunny weather. Across the gunpowder flashed a brilliant flock of black-and-white birds of the skua family that had been feeding on the foreshores. From the sandbar came the barking of seals.

We waved to the courteous van Delden, who trimmed the sheets of his *Dadeldo* to reach Bensersiel before *die Watten* rose under his keel as the tide ebbed.

At the floating dock of the Langeoog Yacht Verein (yacht club), *Chief,* which from its launching has tended toward a port list, began to list more alarmingly than ever. I transferred the primary tool chest, a box of tinned sardines, and the library to starboard, to little effect. Lisa meanwhile helped an incoming, 36-foot steel sloop, *Vagabund* of Cologne, to tie up in the next berth. I tried to decipher the *Hochundniedrigwasserzeittafeln* again, quite determined now to follow the saplings inside the islands to Holland, in short bursts at high tide when there was enough water in the channels. Van Delden had advised us to leave on the afternoon high of the following day to reach the island of Nordeney via Baltrum.

In the morning, there was a discreet tap on the hull, and something fell into the cockpit. Lisa peered out from under the hatch and retrieved a still-hot package of bread rolls, courtesy of *Vagabund*'s crew. Toni and Mareliz had been to the island's township on their folding bicycles and were donating some of their haul.

Thanking them later, I noticed that our list had disappeared. Toni laughed. "You have been on the sands already!" When I asked why *Vagabund* had been unaffected by the outgoing tide, he explained that it had bilge keels and a draft of only three feet. "It was built on Nordeney, to the conditions here."

After breakfast, Lisa and I strolled through green meadows and poplar-shaded lanes to the town. No motor vehicles were allowed on the island roads. The descendants of a handful of wreckers had built the ocean side of the island into a modern *kurbad* ("spa") featuring an enclosed pool with simulated, four-foot-high breakers for *kurgäste* (guests) who could or would not brave the North Sea. After an unsuccessful attempt to shop—all stores in the little town were closed between noon and three p.m.—we returned to the harbor and had the local specialty, raw herring, pumpernickel bread, and onion, served on the yacht club porch by the club waiter.

At four p.m., we cast off and were joined by *Vagabund,* with Toni offering to act as pilot to Nordeney. We accepted.

Vagabund reached off into *die Watten,* leaving the pricks to starboard. Like markers for a snowbound road, they ran into the

92

distance and disappeared in the gunpowder haze. The *Wattenmeer* otherwise was undistinguishable from the open sea.

We were halfway to Baltrum, reaching in a brisk easterly, when *Chief* began to move sluggishly. I cranked up the engine and dragged the keel through the sands past a few more saplings, cursing van Delden, "local knowledge," and pilots in general. Coinciding exactly with the recommended high-water time for passage, *Chief* lurched to complete halt in a massive bank in the middle of the supposed channel.

Lisa resignedly dropped the sails, and we began to guy out the boom for sit-out leverage. *Vagabund* had observed our situation and came rounding back. "Not much water here," I shouted accusingly. "So it seems," Toni answered and passed a two-inch Dacron tow hawser. Mareliz jumped over to us to tend the tiller while Lisa and I went out on the boom. Lisa held back. "Come on," I said.

"I don't think the topping lift is secured," she said. I jumped out on the boom to demonstrate that it was. It let go, and I fell in. The water went only to my chest.

With the main halyard shackled to the end of the boom, we tried again, with Lisa joining me. *Chief* heeled accordingly, and Toni gave full throttle to his eighty-horsepower Daimler-Benz engine to pull us through. A groan issued from our forward cleat as the six cylinders raced, and we began to move by fractions, then stopped, then started again. The towline vibrated like a steel wire about to snap.

Half an hour and only three saplings later, we came to water deep enough so that we just dragged occasionally. Lisa and I climbed back in the boat. Toni, speaking like a storybook Indian, had an explanation for the shallow part we'd traversed. "Wind is blowing water from the land," he said. "In *die Watten* you read from Nature's book."

Mareliz, glancing at my soaked clothes, compassionately suggested a hot shower and night quarters on Baltrum rather than pressing on to Nordeney on a falling tide. After berthing in the sandy Baltrum lagoon, she even stood a *Kartoffelpuffer* dinner, and

we began to feel rather content, having avoided what I thought of as disaster and shipwreck on the dropping tide.

Baltrum town, as a morning walk to the bakery revealed, was newly built brick, with guest quarters for summer visitors in every house. One or two old skipper's cottages from an earlier era remained, their sloping roofs aligned with the predominating winds and their walls completely sheltered by being in a ditch below the level of the island. On the beach, visitors renting cabanas were duplicating the practice, renting shovels to throw up walls around their *strandkörbe*.

As I began to draw a fine old house set back from the beach, an old couple of the island walked slowly past, their characteristic wedge-shaped eyes surveying me with good humor. The island brogue, which is almost as close to English as it is to German, was strong when the woman spoke. "You are truly drawing the right thing," she said. The man, with his visored skipper's cap and nautical-cut woolen pea jacket, nodded and said, "What we have loved all our lives they are now crowding or demolishing."

Lisa, meanwhile, had had a morning shower, observed by an inquisitive cottontail. She also had topped up on fresh water and Maltz-bier, like the good crew she is, and we were ready to go.

The inside passage to Nordeney along the saplings passed without a brush on the sands, and as we entered the harbor in the wake of *Vagabund*, we conceived a foolish notion that we knew *die Watten* and their game.

The sea spa of Nordeney, with memories of Kaiser Bill and Bismarck, is reminiscent of Brighton, Ostend, or Ocean City, New Jersey, with grand hotels lining the beachfront and the humbler boarding houses grouped behind. On the beach, there were hundreds of colorful cabanas, and farther along, the popular F.K.K. (*freikörperkultur*, or "nudist") beach. Several people were actually swimming in the sea, an unusual sight at the other beaches.

Two hours before high tide on the following day, we were off with *Vagabund* again, making for Borkum, the last in the chain of the East Frisian Islands, and our real discovery of the sands. The gunpowder on the horizon closed in, and past a few dozen saplings

94

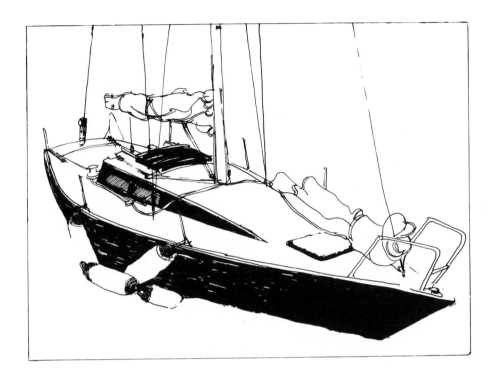

on the approach to Borkum through Horns Balje, dense fog shrouded us completely. *Vagabund*'s foghorn sounded somewhere ahead. "We're stuck," Toni shouted hollowly across the waters. "Press on." As we could not see the next sapling, I ignored this advice and tied the bow line to the sapling next to us, to give *Chief* some haft in the disappearing world. After a few minutes, Toni came paddling over in his folding dinghy. "You'll dry out," he said. "Don't worry; it is nothing."

We did worry, a lot. I rigged an elaborate system of fenders on the starboard side and dragged them down along the hull on lines passed under the bow and stern. Toni helped, chuckling a little. "But it is soft," he said. The fog slowly cleared, and we saw *Vagabund* a hundred yards away, already resting, perfectly level, on her bilge keels.

Mile after mile of sandbars, glistening dully in colors from raw sienna to burnt sepia, began to rise around us as the waters were changed into a vast plain, alive with rivers and oceans of its own. Imperceptibly, *Chief's* keel settled, and we began to heel. With all hands to starboard, she fell to the fendered side, but slowly, dreamlike, and without prospect of damage. The angle of heel, after going beyond what she would provide when knocked on her beam ends at sea, made moving around on deck acutely uncomfortable. Below, it was a great strain to do the simplest task. Blundering about, seeking a foothold, I stepped on and broke the retainer batten in front of the stove.

As soon as the water was shallow enough for wading, we made our way over to *Vagabund.* It was an immense relief to step down on the level sands. The sunlit waters were teeming with life. At every step, crabs would tickle our bare feet and clouds of shrimp danced at our ankles. On every square yard of sandy surface, sand worms had left scores of ringlets, sand processed and divested of micro-organisms. Razorbills were flying low on humming wings, flashes of black and white, scanning pools and rivulets.

Man encroached on *die Watten*, too. From the fog wall in the direction of Borkum a man emerged, carrying an orange plastic bucket like a beacon. He turned out to be a florid, middle-aged rating from the Borkum navy base, out to gather mussels on his day off. Generously, he showed us a bank near the boats where we could collect them by the shovelful before filling his own bucket and fading off into the gunpowder-fogged horizon once more. With Mareliz and Toni, we proceeded to scrape and brush the black mussel shells down to a rich dark blue.

While the haul cooked in a tin bucket on *Vagabund*, Lisa and I

" VACABUND " ON HORNS BALJE

gave the careened *Chief* a scrubbing where she lay, helpless and out of her element, on an island not much longer than herself. And we ran back in loose arcs across the flats and draining rivulets like truant children. The rich smell of the sands was in our nostrils, and the atmosphere around us was charged with luminosity from a deep blue sky overhead. In one of the loneliest stopping places on our journey, high on Horns Balje, we wanted to shout for joy, and we dug our hands into the sands, feeling the magic of life, big and small, more intensely than ever before.

97

PLANS AND COMMENTARY

Svennungsson's Eka

For August Svennungsson's eka, there were no plans. August's son, Bror, who returned to Marstrand to design double-ender fishing boats after spending many years with large production fiberglass and wood boatbuilders such as Storebro Bruk, chuckled and scratched the back of his head when eka drawings were mentioned to him.

"I cannot even recall the beam," he said. "The length overall was fourteen feet and three thumbs (a Swedish boatbuilder's way of saying fourteen feet three inches), because we bent the keel plank to a "filly" (contour jig) that had been fixed at that length.

"The main dimensions came about from the amount of inside room needed in a boat. There had to be leg room between the thwarts, and the need for a good rowing position and stability dictated the beam. My father had a head to himself and did not formulate those things over night.

"I well remember helping him build Konrad's eka. We used to finish them bright or even tarred, but local men like Konrad of course wanted them *trä-ren* (literally 'wood clean,' without finish)."

Shown here is the G.K.S.S. eka. It was drawn in 1949 by the Ohlsson brothers, based on Orust, an island north of Marstrand, to standardize the sailing ekas from many different builders on the west coast of Sweden. The dimensions are similar to a Svennungsson eka but the rig was changed to Bermudian and a keel was added.

—Frank Rosenow

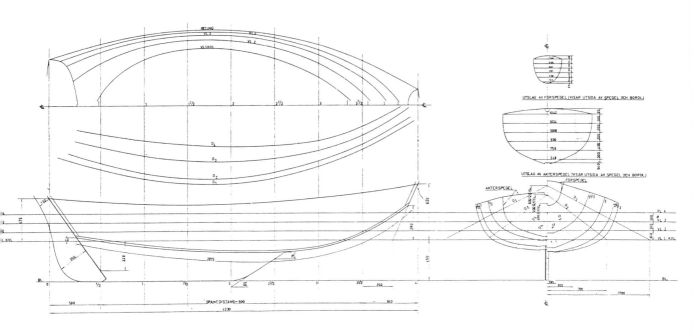

Kratos

LOA:	52′2″
LWL:	34′5″
Beam	12′9″
Draft:	7′2″
Sail area:	1,291.2 sq ft

Kratos was drawn by Albert Andersson, a ship-building engineer who at the time of her creation was Sweden's most successful skerry cruiser designer. He left no writing about her, but it is with the flourish of a bygone age, that, apart from the smooth lines, he marks up a separate saloon for women on the interior plan.

—**Frank Rosenow**

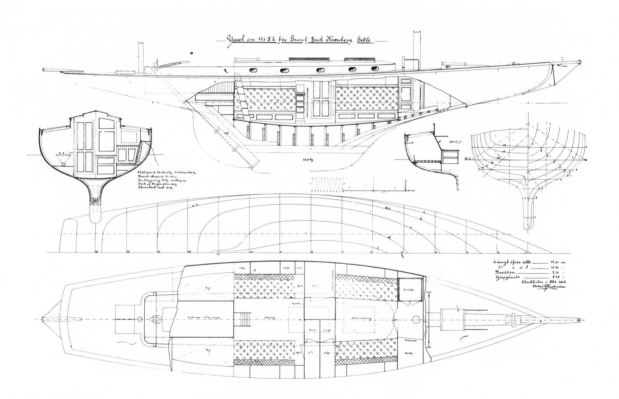

Nordic Folkboat

LOA:	25'
LWL:	19'8"
Beam:	7'2"
Draft:	3'11"
Freeboard:	1'10"
Iron keel:	2,248.7 lbs
Displacement:	4,739.9 lbs
Sail area:	258.2 sq ft

The Nordic Folkboat was drawn up on the basis of preliminary drawings I had made in 1941. The definitive drawings were completed in November of that year on the prompting of Sven Salén and the Royal Swedish Sailing Association. The prototype, F-S-1, was built immediately by the highly reputed Arendal yard. I sailed her for the first time on April Fool's Day, 1942, and saw that she was a very handy boat.

The Folkboat was intended, above all, as an inexpensive and seaworthy weekend cruiser for family sailing. I therefore drew a boat with what was for its day spacious belowdecks accommodations. The hull lines reflected the spacious interior at a time when most of the purely recreational sailing boats in Swedish waters were long, narrow skerry cruisers with claustrophobic accommodations.

The interior was simple, with two bunks and a cupboard. A spare bunk and the pantry box ended up in the cockpit, which therefore required a canvas cover.

I chose the lapstrake building method because it was cheaper than carvel planking and would thus keep the price down. Lapstrake planking is strong and also requires less care than carvel planking.

For the rest, except for the stern, the boat was conceived and built in a traditional manner, with the steam-bent frames, keel plank, stem- and sternpost, and floors all made out of oak. The hull planking was Nordic pine. The deck was made from native spruce planking and covered with cotton canvas in the manner of the day to stop leaks.

The mast came from solid native spruce, and I stayed it in a simple manner, with two shrouds, a forestay, and a backstay, adding a jumper strut up top for stability. In spite of the simple rigging, failures have been very rare, and when they do occur, it has been because of carelessness of some sort.

The initial series of sixty boats were sold individually for the Swedish equivalent of $620, including sails. Today, the price of a Nordic Folkboat made in the same manner is about $15,000.

I sailed and owned Nordic Folkboats for fifteen years. Since those days, I have sailed a great many different types of boats. Now I am returning to the Folkboat because she is reliable and can easily be sailed and maintained by one man. Because of the high cost of wood boats, my boat will probably be from the current production series in fiberglass.
—Tord Sundén

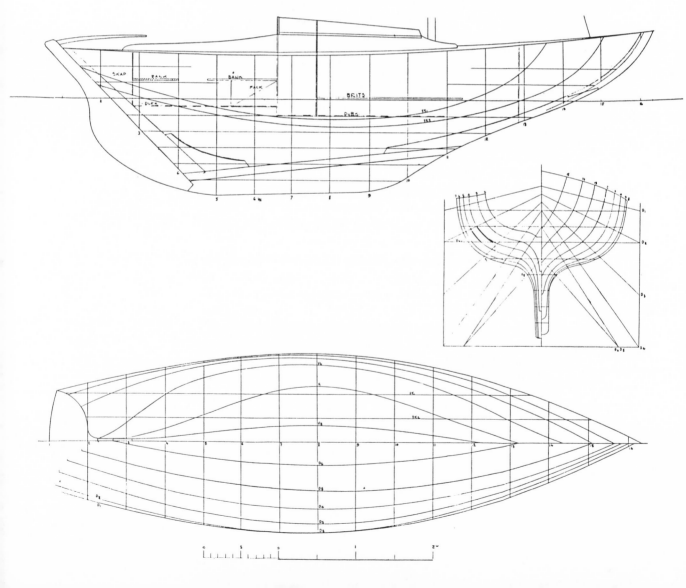

Tumlaren

LOA:	27'3"
LWL:	21'10"
Beam:	6'6"
Draft:	4'2"
Freeboard:	1'8"
Displacement:	3,968.3 lbs
Lead keel:	2,039.3 lbs
Sail area:	215.2 sq ft

The Tumlaren was designed in 1933 as a marriage of the old Koster tradition with the more extreme skerry cruisers of her day. Those were different times, when men worked from Monday morning to Saturday evening, with one week of vacation per year. People were interested in daysailers with stiffness and performance and a reasonable amount of room and comfort. They looked for a feeling of unity with a boat, and the Tumlaren gave it to them, although she was very different from the ordinary run of design at the time.

She was drawn up intuitively. Looking back at her design, I am reminded of the great performance of a moderately beamy boat with smooth lines. My experience of tank testing, which goes back to Bremen in the 1920s, suggests that a test may have some value when applied to smooth water and light air. But in general, the complex variables of sailing cannot be simulated. And the shapes tested rarely point in the right direction anyway.

Müller, my professor in Bremen, used to paint navy barges to a low-visibility pattern he had developed. During World War One, the prescribed paints ran out, and they had to work with what they could find. It later turned out that the haphazard work had a better camouflage record. Maybe yacht design is in the same realm.

The Tumlaren was drawn for carvel wood construction, with fourteen-millimeter planking of Nordic or Oregon pine and a mahogany deck sheer and house. The frames specified are either galvanized steel angles with oak frames between or all oak frames.

The accommodations are Spartan but with full-length transom berths and a locker aft for the galley. The bridgedeck locker houses the stove and cooking utensils. The space under the cockpit floor is used for an icebox.

The first boat was built at Kalle Johansson's in Norrtälje from brown pitch pine that had been aged for nearly a hundred years in a church nearby at Rådmansö. The pitch has greater density than ordinary pine, and when I saw the boat recently, after nearly fifty years, damned if the thing didn't look like new.

Over the years, the Tumlaren has been built in twenty-four countries. I lost count of the numbers around 600, and a lot are being built without authorization. She is a boat of her time, of course, but they are building a mahogany one right now that will be the basis of a fiberglass mold.

Today, the idea in handicap sailboat racing is to draw not a fast boat but a boat with a lower measurement. The International Offshore Rule (IOR) has a kind of triple bonus on beam and hull shapes drawn practically along the measurement points. As the terrible Fastnet Race of 1979 shows, boats drawn to the IOR pitch like mad, trying to shake off their masts and the joinery and equipment down below. A narrower shape would perform better, and if it were not for the Mafia that controls the IOR and our freedom to design, we would get it. For my part, I have for a decade publicly refused to draw boats to the IOR; I do not care to dance with girls that I dislike.   **—Knud Reimers**

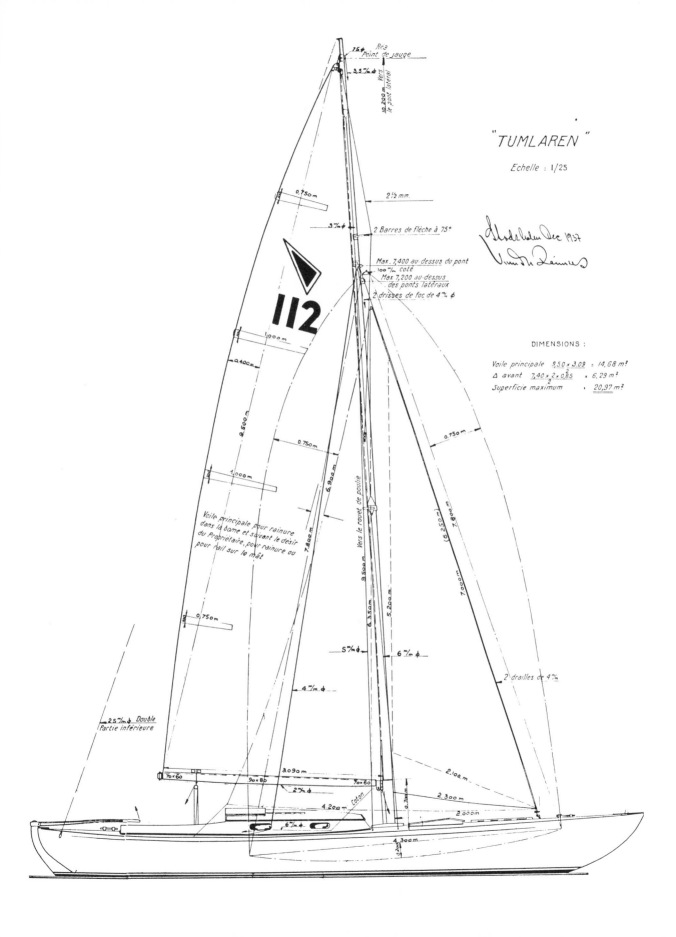

"TUMLAREN"

Echelle : 1/25

Stockholm Dec 1937

DIMENSIONS :

Voile principale   9,50 × 3,09 = 14,68 m²
Δ avant $\frac{7,40 × 2 × 0,85}{2}$ = 6,29 m²
Superficie maximum   = 20,97 m²

"TUMLAREN"

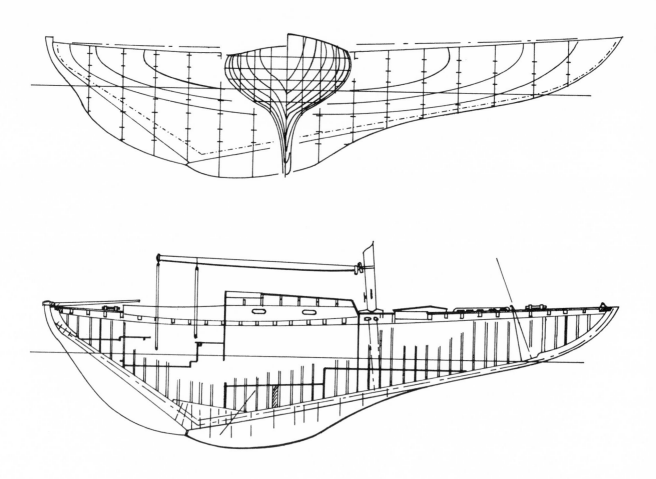

Scampi

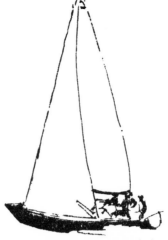

LOA:	29'8"
LWL:	26'2"
Beam:	9'11"
Draft:	4'11"
Displacement:	4,840 lbs

The first *Scampi* was a spontaneous creation, conceived with little regard for measurement rules, for which I had no detailed understanding at the time. I was strongly influenced by the circular underwater shape of racing canoes with their minimum of wetted surface.

I knew what I was after, however. By 1968, most naval architects agreed that a light-displacement hull stabilized by exaggerated beam was potentially faster than a long, narrow hull that depended upon a heavy displacement to counterbalance the press of canvas. I had observed myself that the light, modern hulls behaved better than their Olin Stephens predecessors in rough, offshore conditions. Rather than fighting the waves, the beamy hulls tended to lift over seas, conserving driving power. I wanted to take advantage of that "lift" by moving the driving force in the sails aft, so the sails would effectively push the bow over the seas. It was an intuitive concept, derived perhaps from my tendency to lean back rather than forward in downhill skiing. I wanted *Scampi* to be a "back-leaner," too. But as I whittled away at the hull model to the thirty feet length overall and nine feet of beam of the shape I imagined, it looked pretty terrible. The length-to-beam ratio meant that I had to begin pinching in toward the bow and stern immediately from the point of maximum beam. She was a tub.

But before throwing the model over the side, it occurred to me that the fat could be shaved away below the waterline, straightening out the lines below the turn of the bilge. I put my knife to her from bow to stern.

Holding the model against the sun after the operation and rotating it slowly, the shadows revealed a much sleeker boat. Towing the model on a simple bridle against a likeness of the Fin-gal, one made to scale with weights on the lee rail to simulate heeling, *Scampi* pulled straight and true because of her straighter lines along the bilge, while the Fin-gal consistently swung to windward, wasting energy by trying to break out sideways. Clearly, on a beamy, light-displacement hull, the rounded hull shape is the primary weather heel factor as she heels over.

Scampi's interior drawing differs in substance from the reality on board the first completed boat, which was more Spartan. The deck layout and profile is not the same, and the freeboard has been increased 4½ inches. As usual, the change from a lead keel in the original one-off to a cheaper iron one in the production Scampi meant a small increase in displacement and loss of performance.

—Peter Norlin

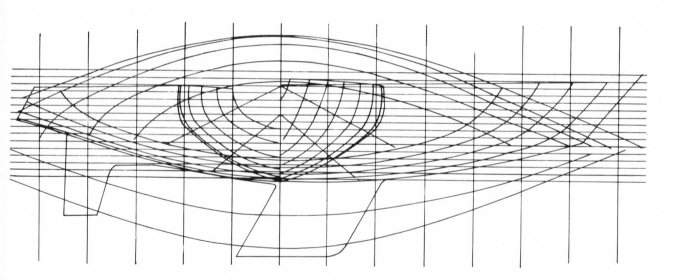

110

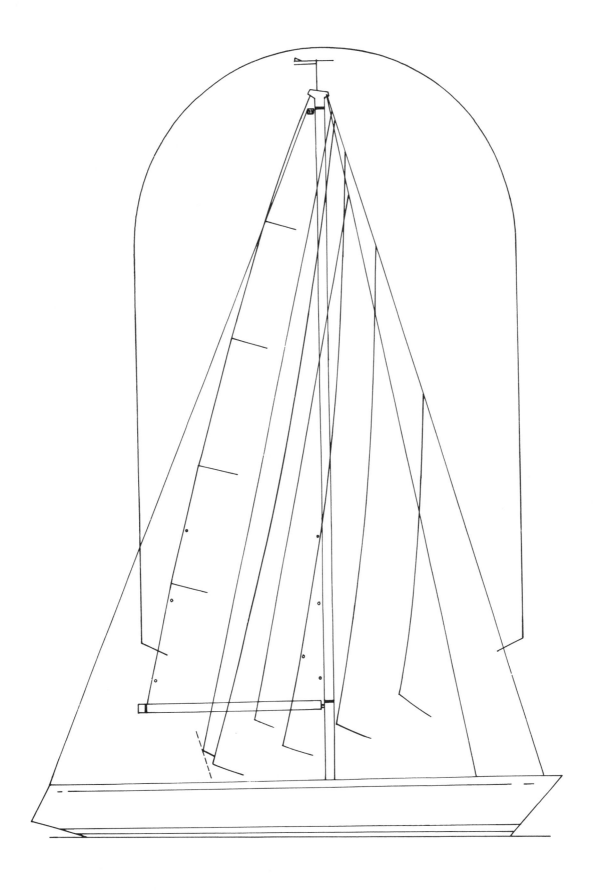

Bris

LOA:	19'8"
LWL:	18'4"
Beam:	5'6"
Draft (with centerboard):	1'7"
(with keel):	3'11"
Freeboard:	2'11"
Displacement:	2,000-2,200 lbs

Ballast: from zero to 275 pounds
with iron bulb keel

Bris was designed to fit through a basement door measuring six feet by two feet nine inches, so she had to be small. In shape, her hull resembles viking ships, whaleboats, and other traditional double-enders, but with a longer waterline.

Bris is of a symmetrical hull shape, as I believe this property has more influence on balance than lateral area. She steered herself through thousands of nautical miles with a locked rudder. The waterline length is maximized, as she is not built to a measurement rule and I consider a long waterline of the utmost importance for a boat's speed and ability to pass through waves. The boat's ability to pass over a wave I consider to be the relation between the rotational momentum and the product of the volume of the reserve displacement and distance to the center of rotation.

Bris served me very well on many stormy ocean passages. She was a fast boat, as exemplified by a St. Helena to Martinique passage of 4,000 miles in forty-five days. So well did she sail that I am now building a modified version, *Bris III,* with the same hull lines, again in cold-molded wood. With the help of a friend and computer software, her form has been changed to include bilge keels and a spritsail. There will also be a large oar of the type traditionally used in China. I still own *Bris I* and plan to sail her in the Swedish and Finnish archipelagos to try out the new spritsail rig.

—Sven Lundin

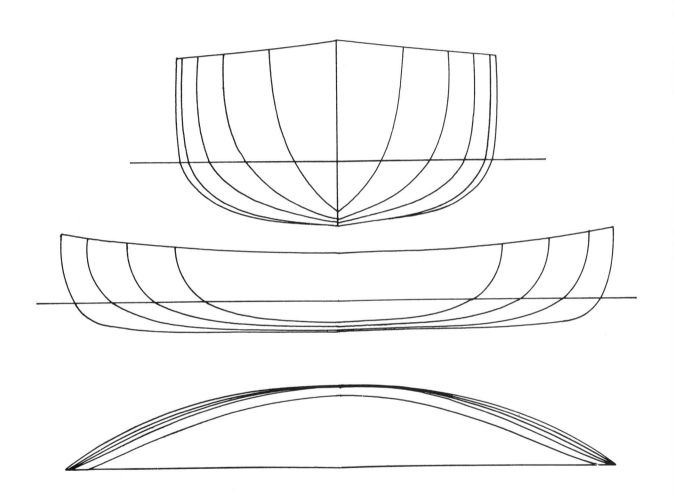

Ganbare

LOA:	34'3"
LWL:	28'6"
Beam:	10'8"
Draft:	6'3"
Displacement:	12,500 lbs

The Ganbare was my entry into boat design; the bulb flashed, you might say! I only got around to analyzing the International Offshore Rule (IOR) a year after I drew her, so she was not a rule boat. At the time, designers had got the proportions all wrong, and I therefore designed a smaller boat with more sail and propulsion.

The other idea I had was to balance the ends right. Other boats had V-shaped entries, which tended to pound when they heeled over, so I designed my entry in the shape of a U that turned into a V when heeled. Instead of a flat, wide stern that would create distortion when heeled over, the Ganbare has a narrow V-shaped stern, which made the boat balance out rather than become cock-eyed when heeling. It was really a double-ender hull that rotated uniformly.

At the stern, other boats usually had a lot of IOR distortion; in trying to distribute volume smoothly, I came up with a bustle and rudder that fit into the hull so it left a very smooth wake and did not throw up any water, especially not to windward. I had already decided that Ton Cup racing was won to windward or offwind. The Ganbare pointed much higher than anything that was around then and really still outpoints a lot of boats. She has a good sea motion.

The keel was deep and thinner than that of other boats of her day, although they are making even thinner ones today. The sweep of her keel was just enough to shed kelp, since there is a lot of that around San Diego. I put a sweep in the rudder, too, for the same reason.

I had only looked at the Rule, but it fit my design ideas anyway, so the boat had to be built. People thought I was crazy. Carl Eichenlaub built her on the cheap, as a kind of throwaway, as I had to pay for her. The hull cost around $20,000 and Murphy & Nye gave me the $6,000 sail inventory on a use-now, pay-later plan. In fact, the sails were to be paid for when the boat was sold.

Country Woman and *Lively* were built to the same plans except for the final glassing of the hull, not done on the original. The original Eichenlaub was fairly sound, structurally.

—Douglas Peterson

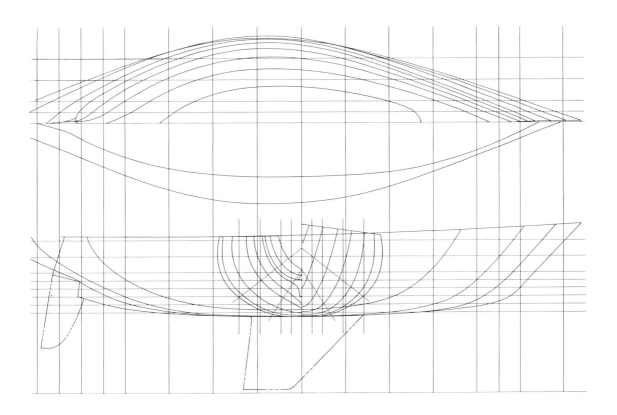

Ganbare

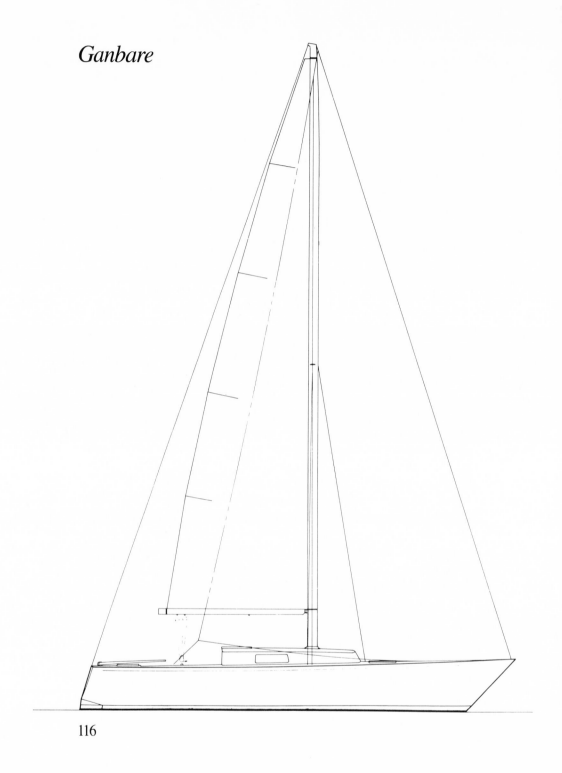

Chief

When my 1974 Quarter-Ton Cup winner, *Accent*, and her subsequent near-sistership, *Chief*, came about, the Ton Cup competition was intense, and I was influenced by designers such as Peterson and, above all, by the International Offshore Rule, with which, by then, I was familiar. The forward depth measurement made me draw displacement to the ends to save *L,* a technical benefit under the rule. I increased displacement by 10 percent from the Scampi to give better *SA,* or wetted surface. A greater prismatic coefficient lowered the center of buoyancy, which required a correspondingly heavier keel to give the same amount of stability. The aft girth station measurement was improved to the extent that *Accent* had an *L* 7¾ inches shorter on essentially the same canoe body. I put the yield into extra sail area. In spite of her being a bit against the grain, *Accent/Chief* was a better boat than the Scampi in smooth water. But the higher prismatic coefficient hurt her performance in a rough seaway, where the Scampi remained an outstanding boat. We saw just how good she was when competing (with an *Accent/Chief* type of keel replacing the original one) at the Half-Ton Cup six years after I drew her. In heavy air, she was still the fastest boat by a good margin.

Frank Rosenow's *Chief* is a general refinement of the thinking that went into *Accent,* the principal difference being a narrower, by nearly two inches, and even longer, straight-lined hull.

Since *Chief,* I have been able to draw some boats for a 1980s market less centered on the IOR—the Express, a Scandinavian one-design class in the J/24 style, and the fast cruiser Nova, to mention two. They are a bit shallower forward, and I have tried to cut away bad parts induced by the rule, but in all honesty, there was not much that could be improved.

As does the rule, I try to retain a moderate displacement in any boat. Crew weight on the rail is a large factor in the stability of a smaller craft, but it is wrong to market a boat for cruising that needs five heavyweights to windward to stand up to a breeze.

—Peter Norlin

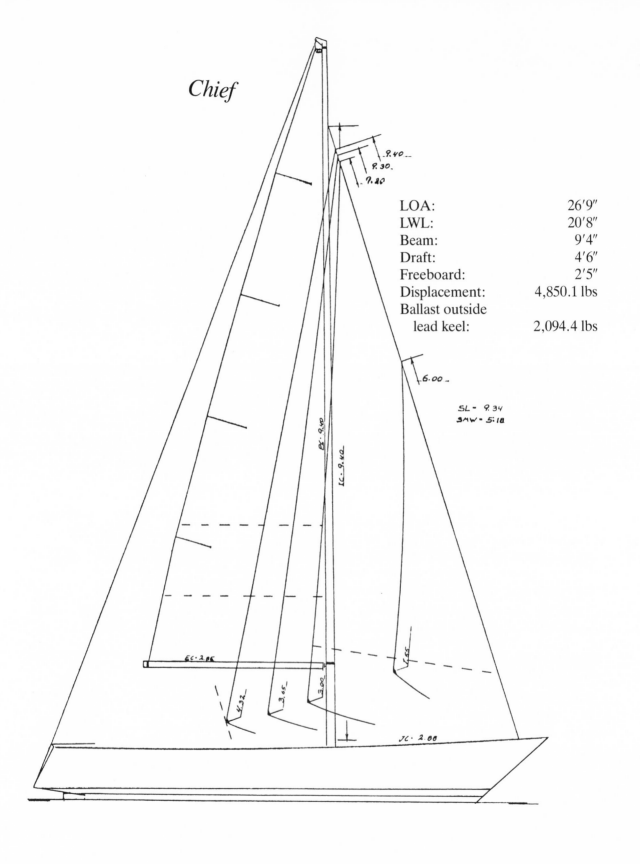

Chief

LOA: 26′9″
LWL: 20′8″
Beam: 9′4″
Draft: 4′6″
Freeboard: 2′5″
Displacement: 4,850.1 lbs
Ballast outside
 lead keel: 2,094.4 lbs

Freedom 40

The Freedom 40 began with my desire for a swift, simple boat that I could singlehand through the Caribbean islands. I wanted free-standing masts because I felt that the strains and complexities of wire rigging were as unnecessary on sailboat masts as they had proven to be on airplane wings. Jibs were out because they were troublesome upwind and inefficient offwind. A divided rig was desirable to make things more manageable and to keep the boat in balance downwind by simply winging out each sail on opposite sides. A large, open cockpit in the center of the boat was called for because the cockpit's where you spend most of your time in the Caribbean.

With these requirements in mind, I went to Halsey Herreshoff, a very capable naval architect, who provided fine traditional lines and some excellent general advice. For example, the wishbone boom feature came right from the Herreshoff Museum, which he maintains in Bristol, Rhode Island.

Happily enough, the Freedom 40, which resulted from these deliberations, proved to be a very able sailer. I guess it was no accident that the Freedom 40 in many ways resembles some of the practical island craft and trading schooners that I observed during my many years in the Caribbean.　　　　　**—Garry Hoyt**

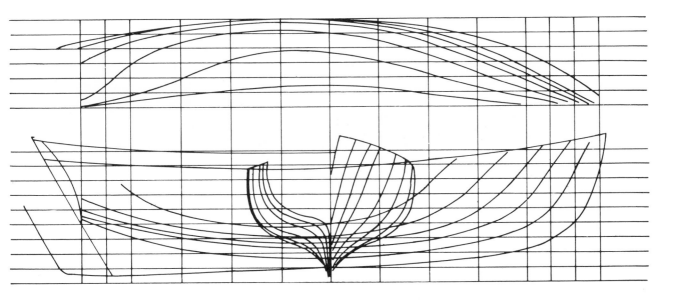

120

Wiåka

LOA:	19'8"
LWL:	19'6"
Beam:	4'3"
Draft (board up):	1'1"
(board down):	3'1"
Ballast: lead center-	
board casing	617.3 lbs
Freeboard:	1'1"
Displacement:	1,322.7 lbs
Mainsail:	93.8 sq ft
Jib:	43.6 sq ft

For *Wiåka,* the authentic builder's drawings have been lost, but in the file of the late designer Sven Thorell at the Maritime Museum in Stockholm, I found an approximation: Design 120. It was drawn up formally a long time after *Wiåka* was built, on the occasion of a rule change for D Class sailing canoes, but it corresponds to her in dimensions and arrangements, with the exception of a greater beam and less ballast lead.

Thorell did not comment on the design, but in the pamphlets on canoe building that he wrote, he is seen as a great purist who preferred a hypersensitive, unballasted sailing canoe to the comparatively stable *Wiåka*, a type that he referred to, deprecatingly, as "almost a boat"! Writing about canoe cruising, he did admit that ballast could be a useful ingredient, even if it did spoil a little of the fingertip sensitivity of an unballasted craft.

"Cruising," he wrote at the time of *Wiåka*'s conception, "is surely the finest type of canoeing. It gives you a chance to cast off the masquerade costume of civilization. I can think of no better way to come close to nature than in a shallow-draft canoe that can sail where no other boat may follow but is equally safe in open water."

Wiåka's owner, Bengt Möllerström, backs up her seaworthiness. "If she is capably trimmed, fitted with a cockpit sack (an eskimo-developed, waterproof piece of skin or canvas that fits around the cockpit and sailor to prevent water from entering the boat), and one of Fredrik Ljungström's storm sails (without battens and hollow-leeched), she can weather sixteen or seventeen meters per second, even in open water."

Wiåka was built by E. Hammarlund in 1936, with eight-millimeter pine planks on steam-bent oak frames 4½ inches apart. She won the Swedish D Class canoe championships in 1952, sailed by Gösta Hammarlund.

—**Frank Rosenow**

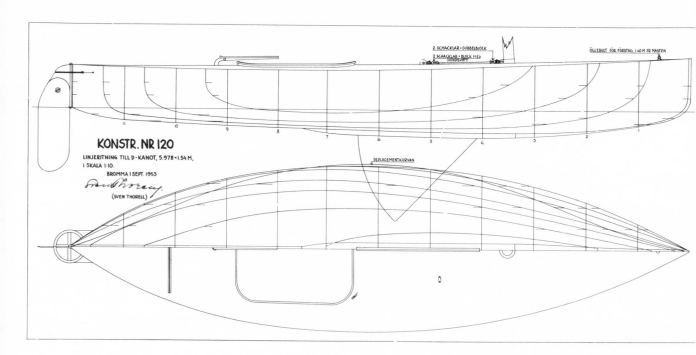

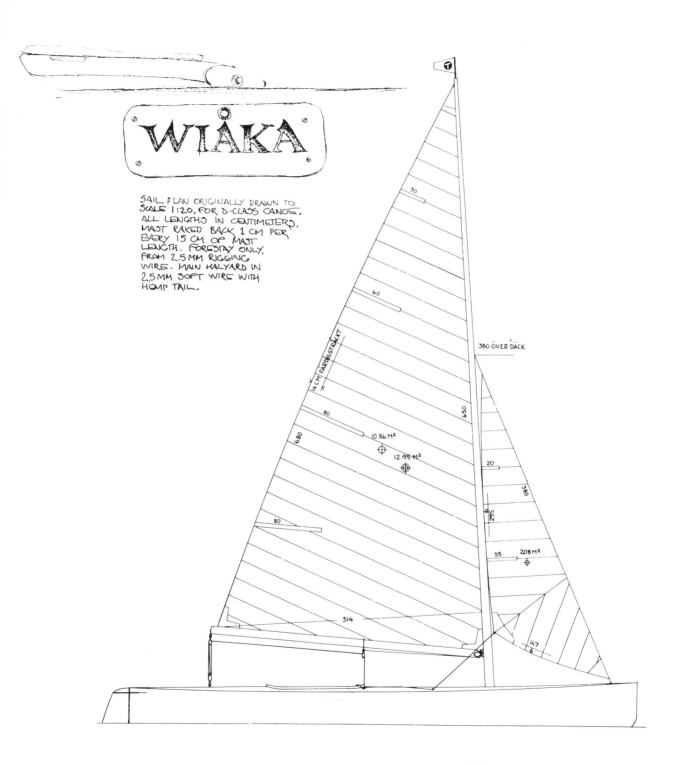

WIAKA

SAIL PLAN ORIGINALLY DRAWN TO
SCALE 1:20. FOR D-CLASS CANOE.
ALL LENGTHS IN CENTIMETERS.
MAST RAKED BACK 1 CM PER
EVERY 15 CM OF MAST
LENGTH. FORESTAY ONLY.
FROM 2.5 MM RIGGING
WIRE. MAIN HALYARD IN
2.5 MM SOFT WIRE WITH
HEMP TAIL.

30

60

380 OVER DECK

650

14 CM FARD/STRAKT

80

680

10.86 M²

12.95 M²

20

580

295

35   208 M²

80

314

147
6

The Colin Archer

LOA:	36'8"
LWL:	34'5"
Beam:	12'5"
Draft:	5'8"
Displacement:	26,455.2 lbs
Inside pig iron:	12,133 lbs

The Klädesholmen Colin Archer was built without any plans, and I hope supporters of the general type will agree when I consider her a unique boat to which a substitute set of plans would bear little relation.

—Frank Rosenow

Author's Comment

In the 1930s, the Swedish steam locomotive designer Professor Fredrik Ljungström developed a thick, unstayed mast that could be roller-reefed by rotation, the loose-footed, double cat sail flopping out wing-and-wing on a run. Using wood, the mast had to be pretty substantial at the base, as did the cog-wheel arrangement he designed to turn it below deck. The designer's son, Professor Olle Ljungström, told me a few years ago that he was still trying to find ways to remedy what he and some others considered the rig's only weakness: a performance loss when reaching because of excessive twist in the sail. With the Herreshoff wishbone, material improvements, and promotion, the present gradual acceptance of such rigs would no doubt have cheered the old man, who saw no such thing in his lifetime.
—Frank Rosenow

125

126

About the Author

Frank Rosenow was born in Jannowitz, in the lower Silesian Mountains, in 1944. To escape wartime Europe, his family moved to Marstrand, Sweden, a small seafaring town where his mother grew up. There, at the age of five, Rosenow learned to sail a traditional Swedish eka. Since that time, he estimates he has spent a third of his life afloat in everything from racing dinghies to offshore yachts. Rosenow learned the craft of sailmaking at the last traditional sail loft in Sweden. He has worked as a journalist for the *Sydney Daily Telegraph* and the Associated Press. According to Mr. Rosenow, the only thing he enjoys more than sailing is drawing, one of the few activities that still ties him to the shore.

Acknowledgments

Thanks to Bror Svennungsson, Tord Sundén, Knud Reimers, Peter Norlin, Sven Lundin, Doug Peterson, and Garry Hoyt, who generously added lines plans and commentaries at the back of the book. Thanks, too, to W.W. Norton & Co., Inc., for permission to use some of my drawings first published in *Manual Art*.